MACRAME FASHIONS AND FURNISHINGS

Macrame
Fashions and Furnishings

by
Charles Barnes
and
David P. Blake

IN COLLABORATION WITH
WILLIAM BAKER

Hearthside Press, Inc. Publishers
Great Neck, New York 11021

Contents

1. Materials and Methods 9

2. Basic Cords, Knots and Patterns 39

3. Projects 61

SOURCES OF SUPPLY 251

INDEX 253

OUR GRATEFUL ACKNOWLEDGEMENTS TO

Canadian editor and handicrafts expert, William Baker, for his invaluable assistance in editing, for developing a number of projects and project diagrams and for his helpful criticism in the preparation of this book.

Also to Joseph Ratke, for the photographs, all made especially for *Macrame Fashions and Furnishings*.

1

Materials and Methods

The basic tools and materials for macrame are simple, few in number and readily available to everyone interested in knotting. They include knotting boards, clamps, pins, tape measure, rubber bands and cutting shears. While there are tools and materials specifically for macrame, which will make knotting easier—lacking these, any number of substitutes may be found, probably right in your own home.

For example, an ideal surface for knotting is a composition board known as Homosote. However, this does not mean that it is the only material which may be used and in this chapter we have included a number of good substitutes, such as foam pillow, corrugated cardboard, acoustic tile and bulletin boards. Knotting materials range from common jute to the most interesting of the man-made fibers. Always keep in mind the ultimate purpose of your project and select your tools and materials accordingly.

In this chapter, we have outlined various working methods which will simplify the handling of the cords to be knotted, and produce satisfactory results. However, you will find that individual requirements may cause you to depart from or adapt the methods explained. As long as your technique produces competent knots, and is comfortable to work with, you should not hesitate to substitute your own methods. Since materials and individual working habits vary greatly, we have included only basic knotting and knotting techniques. By all means, experiment. You will probably be surprised and delighted with your own creations.

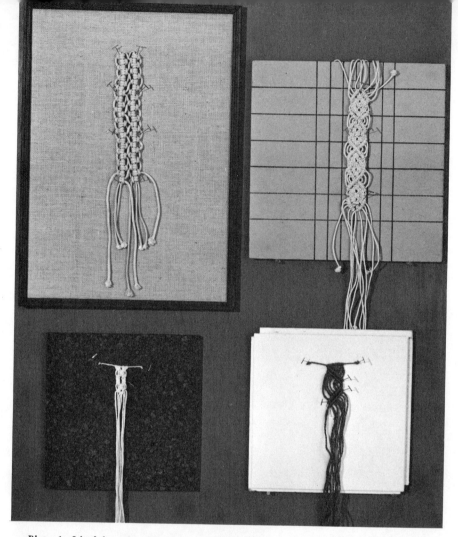

Plate 1. Ideal knotting boards made from bulletin boards, composition boards, cork tiles or acoustic tiles.

KNOTTING BOARDS
(Plate 1)

A knotting board serves several purposes. It provides a stable base upon which cords may be fastened at the beginning of and during a project. As the work progresses, the knotting board will continue to be the working area with completed portions being unpinned and moved up and off the board out of the way. Guidelines marked on the knotting board will also help you arrange symmetrical patterns and measure off portions of the project as the knotting progresses.

COMPOSITION BOARD
(Plate 1)

Composition board is perhaps the most practical, available and inexpensive material you can use as a knotting surface. It is light, durable and portable. Most lumberyards carry a variety of such materials for insulation and other construction purposes. Usually, it is not necessary to purchase a large sheet of this material. Most lumberyards will cut a piece to your specifications for a nominal sum. Before selecting any composition board, however, check to make sure that it is not the type that flakes easily or will color off on your knotting, your hands or your clothing. When you have completed your macrame projects, the composition board may be covered with burlap or other loose-weave fabric and serve as an attractive and useful bulletin board.

ACOUSTIC TILES
(Plate 1)

Inexpensive acoustic tiles will give you a precut and ready-to-use composition board. Usually, tiles are available in 12-inch and 24-inch squares and 24-inch by 48-inch rectangles. Tiles, having a porous or pin-perforated surface, should be avoided since the holes may interfere with your pinning. Acoustic tiles, when no longer needed for knotting, may also be covered with fabric and used as a handy bulletin board.

BULLETIN BOARDS
(Plate 1)

Bulletin boards will make very convenient knotting surfaces. Most are framed and have a firm backing, providing a strong working surface. Since the boards have been manufactured to accommodate pins, the surface will be most suitable to macrame.

Dark cork, in self-adhesive squares and strips, may also be used. However, because cork by itself is rather flexible; masonite, plywood or lumber may have to be applied as additional backing. The combination, though, will make a firm and portable knotting surface.

FOAM RUBBER SQUARES
(Plate 2)

Foam rubber squares (sold as pillow fillers) can be used as adequate knotting surfaces. To provide the necessary "board" consistency, the foam

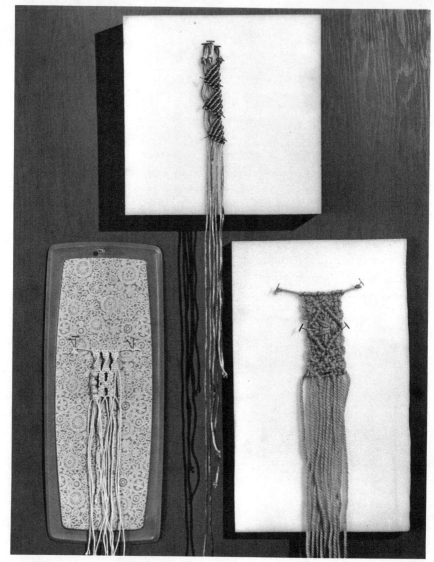

Plate 2. Satisfactory knotting boards made from foam rubber pillow fillers, foam rubber upholstery padding or rubber kitchen pads.

rubber should be at least 2-inches thick. This will permit you to insert pins deep enough to withstand the tension placed upon the cords during knotting. Foam rubber mattresses, bolsters or chair cushions may also be used. If these are fabric-covered, the macrame pinning may be done right into the fabric, but use pins small enough in diameter not to damage the fabric cover. Excess tension exerted on the pins may stretch the fabric out of shape.

Foam Rubber Padding
(Plate 2)

Foam rubber upholstery padding, usually measured in ¼-inch to 2-inch thicknesses will also make a satisfactory knotting surface. Since this material is generally sold by the foot, small quantities, suitable to your needs, can be purchased. Its relative thinness will, however, require some form of backing —such as several layers of corrugated cardboard, glued or taped together.

Rubber Pads
(Plate 2)

Rubber pads, sold in variety stores, will provide a satisfactory working surface. The pads should be sufficiently thick to keep the pins in place when tension is placed upon them. When working with this kind of knotting surface, as with all thin surfaces, you should exercise care that the pins do not penetrate all the way through, scratching table surfaces or whatever is underneath. If the rubber pad you buy is too thin and flexible, you can add a backing of layers of corrugated cardboard taped or glued together.

Corrugated Cardboard
(Plate 3)

A very handy and inexpensive knotting board can be made by gluing together several layers of corrugated cardboard. For added strength, they should be glued with the grain of the cardboard reversed for each layer. Again, make certain that your pinning does not penetrate the cardboard to mark or scratch your worktable surface.

Clipboard
(Plate 3)

A clipboard will serve as one of the most portable of all knotting boards. It can easily be balanced in your lap and is firm enough to provide a solid base. It can be covered with a variety of materials suitable to accept pinning. As an example, a terry cloth towel may be folded and fastened under the clip, the towel providing a medium for the pins, and the board supplying a firm working support. Or, if you prefer, your clipboard may be covered with several layers of corrugated cardboard or foam padding.

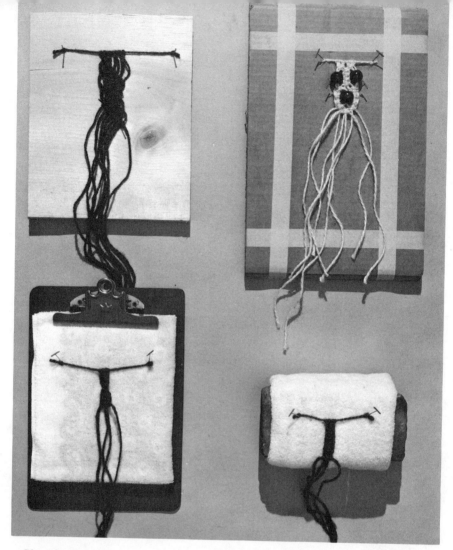

Plate 3. *Makeshift knotting boards may be made from a wood board, layers of corrugated cardboard taped together, toweling placed on a clipboard or toweling wrapped around a brick.*

BRICKS
(Plate 3)

For very small projects or long and narrow pieces, you can cover bricks with several layers of terry cloth toweling. The toweling will hold the pins and the brick will provide a weighted base. It should be noted, though, that the one disadvantage to this "knotting board" is the small work surface. The cords being knotted can not lie directly on the knotting surface as with other larger materials. When cords are held some distance from the knotting surface, equal tension control is much more difficult. Your work will also have a tendency to become slightly off-balance, which would disrupt your knot patterns.

WOODEN BOARDS
(Plate 3)

As a substitute, a wooden board may be used for knotting. It should be of the soft variety, such as pine. Pins may not be strong enough to penetrate the wood and you may have to use very thin finishing nails instead. This will involve using a hammer to insert and extract the nails, which is both cumbersome and time-consuming.

BOARD SIZES

Personal preference and the scale of your project will largely determine the "correct" size of your knotting surface. Small projects, such as bookmarks, may be worked on boards 9-inches square or smaller. Medium-size or elongated projects, such as bags and belts, may be worked conveniently on surfaces of from 12-inches to 18-inches square. Larger projects, such as vests and wall hangings, should be worked on boards large enough to accommodate the entire width of the project. One medium-size board, approximately 12 inches by 18 inches, will accommodate most projects. The cords may be pinned across the narrow end of the board for long, thin projects and across the wide end, for broader ones. A medium-size board will also have the advantage of allowing you to rest one end in your lap while leaning the head of the board against a table-edge or chair-back. In this case, the project can be held at a comfortable distance and angle for knotting.

MARKING BOARDS WITH GUIDELINES
(Plate 4)

Knots are generally made in regular patterns. Because of the flexibility of some cords, this regularity sometimes becomes difficult to maintain. It is, therefore, helpful to mark the knotting board with guidelines to assist in the placement of the cords and knots. Both vertical and horizontal guidelines should be drawn, the vertical lines acting as guides to the placement of vertical rows of knots and the maintaining of straight edges. The horizontal lines will guide you in maintaining straight lines of knots across the width of the project. You should always remember that it is virtually impossible to straighten a project once it is completed and unless straight lines and proper tensions are maintained throughout the working of the project, the end result will be unsatisfactory.

Using certain knotting boards, you will be able to draw your guidelines directly on the knotting surface. These will probably include composition board, light-colored bulletin boards and other hard-surface, light-colored materials. On others, such as foam rubber, toweling, dark cork and clip-boards, it will be both impossible and impractical to do. In this case, large sheets of paper should be attached to the surface of the board. Guidelines may then be marked on the paper. Draw all guidelines clearly and spaced far enough apart so that when the center portion is covered with cords, you will still be able to follow the lines right across the board. Color coding of the lines might be helpful. That is to say, all lines drawn at 1-inch intervals could be black, those at ½-inch intervals could be red and those at ¼-inch intervals could be blue. This will identify the individual lines crossing the knotting board when the center portion is covered with work in progress. As a rule, lines drawn closer than ¼-inch are not necessary. To save time in drawing your lines, get some large sheets of graph paper from a stationery supply store. They are usually available in sizes up to 18-inches by 24-inches, thereby accommodating most projects. Graph lines are usually drawn at 4, 5 or 6 lines to the inch.

In some projects, such as the Christmas tree, an outline of an entire project may be drawn on the graph paper, before any knotting work is begun, and adjustments made where necessary.

CLAMPS
(Plate 4)

While not essential to simple macrame, various clamps will be of great help in more complicated projects. C-clamps are probably the most versatile available. Because they are adjustable, they will fit varying thicknesses of knotting boards. They can also, where required, be opened wide enough to clamp to tabletops and the combined thicknesses of a knotting board and the tabletop together.

Spring-type clamps can also be used but not having the capacity to open widely, they are more limited than C-clamps. In any case, make sure that the clamps you buy can be opened wide enough to accommodate both knotting board and tabletop thicknesses.

MEASURING CORDS WITH CLAMPS
(Plate 4)

Many projects call for a large number of cords all cut to the same length. Measuring and cutting them, individually, will be both time-consuming and possibly inaccurate. To get around this, you can use a pair of C-clamps and a tabletop.

First establish the length of cord required for your project. Divide this length by half. Place your two C-clamps on the edge of the tabletop using the half measure as the distance between the two clamps. Wrap the cord you wish to cut around the top of the clamps the number of times equal to the total number of cords required. Cut all the cords at one end. All your cutting and measuring is thus accomplished in one simple operation. *For*

Plate 4. Clamps are useful tools for macrame. Cord is measured accurately around two C-clamps (rear). Cords are held taut by C-clamps (left front). The knotting board is held securely to table by large spring clamp (right front).

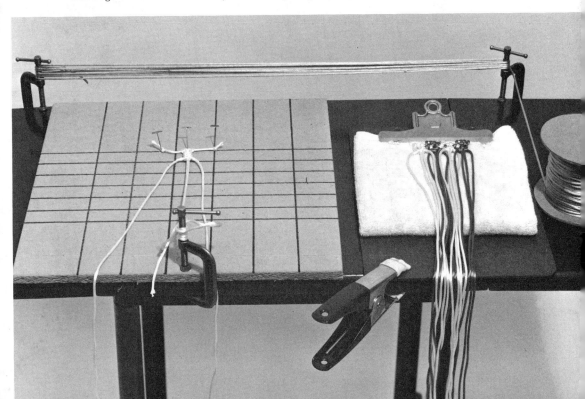

example: Assuming your project requires 40 cords, each 10-feet long, set up your clamps on the table top 5-feet apart. Now, wind your cord around the tops of the clamps 40 times. Cut all the cords at one end and you will have 40 cords of 10-feet each.

If the length of the cord required is more than twice as long as any available surface, you will have no alternative but to measure and cut each cord individually, but your C-clamps will still minimize the time involved and the possibility of error. *For example:* A project requires cords 15 feet in length. Your tabletop is only 6-feet long. Divide the length of the required cord into multiples which you can accommodate on your table. In this case, 3 lengths each of 5 feet will give you the required 15 feet. Place your C-clamps 5-feet apart on the tabletop and wind the cord to be measured 3 times from clamp to clamp. This time do not cut all the cords but only the one leading to the spool or skein where it touches a clamp for the third time. Unwind the cut cord and you will have an accurately measured 15-foot cord ready to use for your project. Repeat as many times as necessary to get all the cords required.

Securing Your Knotting Board with Clamps
(Plate 4)

If you are using a small knotting board, such as a clipboard, you may find it difficult to hold the board securely as you work the knots. In this case, simply attach your knotting board to a convenient tabletop using one of your C-clamps.

Tension on Cords
(Plate 4)

For various knots, you will be required to tie certain cords over core-cords (*see page 40*) and it may be advisable to place a certain amount of tension on this core-cord. To do this, simply place a C-clamp on the edge of your knotting board and attach the core-cords to it. Your hands will then be left free to concentrate on tying controlled knots. For this purpose, you may also use a spring-type clamp, either placing the core-cords under the clamp at the foot of your knotting board, or tying them through the hole in the clamp handle. As your work progresses, the knotted portion can be moved farther away from the clamp and the cord-cords resecured, maintaining equal tension as before.

PINS

Pins are essential to all macrame projects. They secure the initial cords, and as the work progresses, they provide the correct amount of tension and positioning for your cords, thus keeping your work straight and the knotting neat. Large-headed pins are recommended since the knotting process calls for pins to be inserted and withdrawn frequently. Small-headed pins would be hard to handle and uncomfortable to use. Pins should also have a strong shank since they will be carrying a fair tension from the knotting in progress.

PIN SIZES
(Plate 5)

The larger the cord and the bigger the scale of your project, the stronger your pin should be. Consider, also, the diameter of the pin in relation to the type of cord being used. For small woven cords, such as rattail, use small-diameter pins to avoid breaking the surface threads of the cord. For twisted cords or cords with a coarsely-woven surface (such as cotton cable, or nylon seine twine) pinning will require special attention. If a large pin is inserted between the twists of such cords, the tension placed on the cord during knotting may cause the twists to unwind. Not only will this destroy the cord, but it will be impossible to maintain a proper tension on it. Therefore, for twisted cords, insert small-diameter pins directly through the twists. Alternatively, you may knot the cords and insert the pins through the knots. If neither of these procedures seem adequate, wrap a small piece of tapes around the cord and insert the pin through the taped portion.

TYPES OF PINS
(Plate 5)

The most convenient and widely used pins are "T" pins, so named because of their T-shaped heads. The large flat head makes it very easy to handle. They are relatively inexpensive and are usually available in various lengths and diameters. The longer the pin, the larger the diameter.

Large-headed hatpins are strong and easy to use, but since they are rather expensive, any sizable quantity for a large project would be impractical.

Small bulletin board pushpins or map pins can be used with small cords and small-size projects. Their large heads make them easy to handle. With

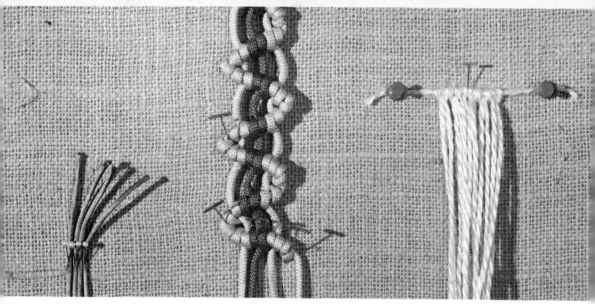

Plate 5. Small cords are pinned to the knotting board before the knotting is begun (left). The knotted piece is pinned as the work progresses (center). The holding-cord (across the top) is pinned to the knotting board before the knotting is begun (right).

very fine yarns, small bulletin board pushpins may be used, but because of their short shanks and large plastic heads, their use is limited. Lacking more suitable equipment, very thin finishing nails can be used. However, they would be satisfactory only for such coarse cords as jute or sisal since the surface twist of these cords is not easily injured. Nails, however, require the use of a hammer which, as we've said, becomes cumbersome.

Common straight pins have only very limited use because the small heads make them difficult to handle. Generally, they are also too flexible to withstand the tension required by macrame knotting.

BEGINNING WITH PINS
(Plate 5)

Cords may be pinned individually, side-by-side, to start a project. They are usually placed along the top of the knotting board and one pin is placed through the center of each cord.

CONTINUING WITH PINS
(Plate 5)

As the knotting progresses, the first pins can be removed, the knotted portion moved up the board and the pins reinserted through several strategic knots. This process is repeated as often as necessary to complete the project. Once the initial knots have been made, however, it is no longer necessary to pin each cord individually. Often, it is not even necessary to insert the pins through the cords at all. Pins placed between the knots and between the cords will be quite sufficient to control the tension and maintain the patterns.

PINNING HOLDING-CORDS
(Plate 5)

To start many projects, cords must be attached to a holding-cord. The knotting-cords are then folded in half and tied, side-by-side, on one horizontal cord. The ends of the holding-cord can then be knotted and pins inserted through the knots at both ends of the holding-cord. This eliminates the need for pinning each cord individually. When many cords are mounted on a holding-cord, it may be necessary to space several pins along the holding-cord to keep the top of the project straight. Then, as work progresses, the original pins can be removed, the knotted portion moved up the board, and new pins inserted in the knotted area to maintain sufficient tension on the knotting-cords.

PINNING RINGS, TUBES, HANDLES, ETC.
(Plate 6)

If the knotting-cords are to be mounted onto something like rings, tubes or handles, these devices should be pinned to the top of the mounting board. If the device you are using is too large or cumbersome to mount directly on the knotting board, the pins may be inserted into the cords adjacent to the point where they are to be tied on the device. Pins may also be placed *around* the mounting device to hold it securely until the first few knots have been tied. Then the pins may be transferred into the knotted portion.

PINNING SYMMETRICAL PATTERNS
(Plate 6)

Frequently, knots or various patterns of knots are repeated in symmetrical patterns. Without the use of pins, this symmetry would be almost impossible to maintain. Guidelines on the knotting board will enable you to place your pins at regular intervals. The cords or knots may then be tied around the

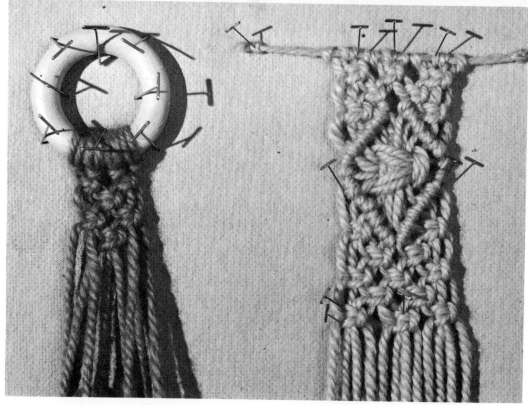

Plate 6. *A ring is secured to the knotting board at the beginning of a project (left). Place pins at strategic points on both the inside and outside to maintain symmetrical patterns as the knotting progresses (right).*

pins as the pattern requires. For example: If the pattern you are working requires a series of knots to be placed an inch apart, by spacing the pins this distance from each other on the knotting board, your pattern knots can then be tied around or below these pins. Frequently a pattern requires that one cord be angled across other cords which are then tied to it. To maintain the proper angle, it may be pinned to the knotting board before the knots are tied. The guidelines, as suggested earlier, will be invaluable in working this type of design. Horizontal rows of knots are particularly dependent on pins placed strategically along a line on your knotting board, since the tension placed on the knots tends to pull your work off the horizontal.

MAKING A BUTTERFLY OR A BOBBIN
(Plate 7)

The knotting process requires cord lengths to be considerably longer than the finished project. Thus a belt which is only 30 inches in length, may require cords at least 4-yards to 5-yards long. Since working with cords of this length would be both impractical and unwieldy, the cords should be wound up in some way, either into "butterflies" or onto bobbins.

To make an efficient butterfly, wind the cord around the little finger and the thumb with the layers crossing over each other in the center. Work from the knotting to the cut end of the cord. If the butterfly has been improperly wound, the cord, as it is pulled loop-by-loop from the butterfly, can easily become entangled.

SECURING THE BUTTERFLY WITH RUBBER BAND OR PLASTIC BAG WIRE ENCLOSURES
(Plate 7)

To secure your butterfly, fasten it with a small, thin rubber band, a paper or plastic-covered wire (the kind used in florist shops or on plastic bags)

Plate 7. Long cords may be shortened to facilitate knotting. Wrap around plastic bobbins (upper left) or homemade cardboard bobbins (upper right). Bundles may be held with rubber bands (lower left) or plastic bag enclosures (lower right).

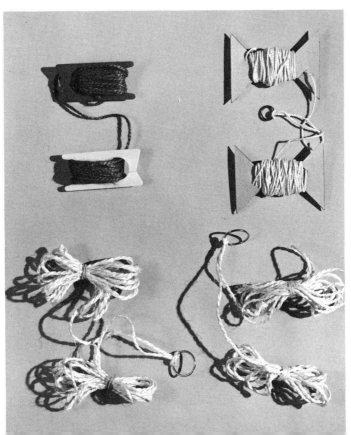

or even with pipe cleaners. As long as the rubber band or wire strip holds the butterfly securely, it can be wound loosely. Tight winding will result in tangling as the cord is pulled free. Whether rubber bands, wire strips or pipe cleaners are used, the cords should not be left wrapped for considerable periods since your cord may well become permanently twisted. If the knotting of your project must be interrupted for any length of time, remove the bands and wire strips and let your cord hang free until knotting is resumed.

BOBBINS
(Plate 7)

Cardboard forms may be cut to make bobbins for your cords. Cut them from substantial pressboard or corrugated cardboard. To determine the right size and weight for your bobbins, consider both the thickness and the length of the project cord. Cut small slits near either end of the bobbin allowing the cord to be inserted and held securely as you knot.

Many art needlework stores carry small plastic bobbins for winding yarn. These are quite suitable for smaller cords. Whichever bobbin is used however, start winding at the cut end and move up the cord to the knotting. The cord may then be conveniently unwound as the work progresses.

TAPE, GLUE, AND WAX
(Plate 8)

Transparent or masking tape will be helpful in your macrame projects. It will work better than pins to start projects using very small cords or yarn. Cords may be spliced and beads threaded with the aid of transparent tape or glue. Frequently, glue may be the only satisfactory means of securing all the loose ends at the conclusion of a project. Both shiny and mat-finish transparent tape can be very helpful. As an example, use shiny tape on cords with a shiny surface (like rattail) and mat-finish tape on a dull surfaced cord.

When using glue, choose one which dries both clear and flexible. Upholstery glues are generally satisfactory. If, as glue dries, it takes on a color of its own, it will detract from the overall effect of your project. If the glue used in splicing is inflexible, the spliced portion of the cord may well end up in the middle of a knot, forcing it out of shape.

BEGINNING WITH TAPE
(Plate 8)

When working with very small cords, yarns or threads, it becomes almost impossible to pin all the cords to the working surface. They may be too small, or there may be too many cords to pin effectively. To get around this, the starter-ends of the cords may be taped together and the ends of the tape pinned to the working surface.

Lay a piece of tape, sticky side up, horizontally across the top of the working surface. Pin down both extremities of the tape. Starting in the center, lay the ends of the cords over the tape, side-by-side, and when all are in position, gently press them into the tape. Then take a second strip of tape, the same length as the first, and with the sticky side down place it over

Plate 8. A broken cord is spliced with upholstery glue (left). Small cords are taped together (upper right) and pinned to knotting board. At lower right, cord ends have been waxed and taped for stringing beads.

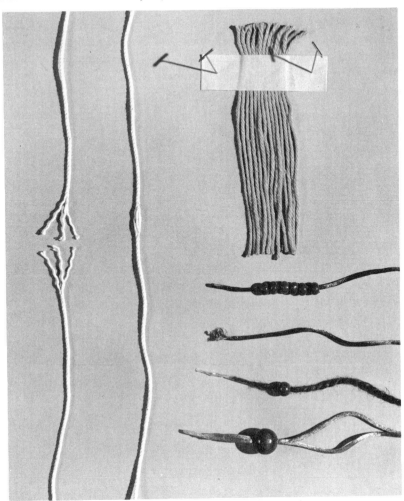

the cords and the first piece of tape, sealing the cords in between the two. Now you can start knotting a short distance below the tape. After knotting is completed, carefully peel the tape from the ends of the cords.

It is not advisable to leave tape on your cords for any extended periods, since in time the glue of the tape may cause the cords to discolor. Better still, is to apply the tape far enough away from the beginning of the knotted area to be able to cut the tape-covered cords off your work and discard them.

SPLICING CORDS WITH GLUE
(Plate 8)

Sometimes cords have to be spliced. A cord may break during the knotting process, or as often happens, cords have been knot-joined during the manufacturing process. If it is inconvenient to join cords with a knot or by gluing, the two ends to be joined may be placed end-to-end and transparent tape wrapped around them. This is the only effective way of joining closely woven cords like rattail.

Glue is best for splicing twisted cords like cable cord. Both ends of the cord should be untwisted about ½-inch to ¾-inch. Apply glue to both frayed ends. Interweave the two ends and twist together in approximately the same degree of twist as the original cord. Allow the glue to dry completely before using the spliced cord for knotting.

THREADING BEADS
(Plate 8)

Using beads in a macrame project may sometimes present a threading problem. Because of the large diameter of many cords and the relatively small holes of the manufactured beads, it is frequently impossible to thread the cord through the needle and if you could, the resulting double strand of cord may not go through the bead.

Also, since cut cord ends tend to fray, this makes bead threading relatively difficult. By wrapping a small piece of tape around the end of the cord, however, it should be possible to thread the tape through the bead. When you apply the tape, leave about ½-inch to ¾-inch of the tape extended beyond the end of the cord. Twist this excess into a small point. Use this point to thread the bead. If there is too much friction between the cord and the inside of the bead, a pair of pliers may help to pull the cord through.

Glue or wax may also be used as an aid to threading beads. Dip ¼-inch to ½-inch of the cord end into glue or wax, squeeze off the excess and allow the cord to hang free until dry. These treated ends will not fray during the work or after it's finished.

ENDING CORDS

Often there is no convenient method for ending a knotting project without having all the cords hang free. The end of a belt with a buckle is a good example. To finish off such a project, carry all the ends of the cord to the reverse side of the belt and secure with glue, eliminating excess bulk.

NEEDLES
(Plate 9)

Tapestry needles, rug needles or yarn darners will come in handy for finishing off various projects. Use these needles with large, elongated eyes with the smaller cords and yarns, to weave carefully back through several knots on the reverse side, to complete a project. The remaining ends should be clipped close, resulting in a clean and smooth finish.

Plate 9. Shears, needles and hooks are helpful tools. They should be just large enough to handle the size of cord being used.

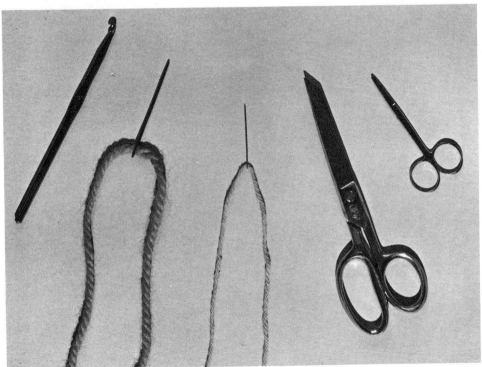

HOOKS
(Plate 9)

Crochet or rug hooks may be used to add cords to the edges of rugs as fringes. New cords may be added to a project in a similar manner. Insert the hook through the rug squares or knotted project and attach the loops to the hook and pull it through. Tie the fold of the cord with a Clove Hitch, then proceed with your knotting as desired.

SHEARS
(Plate 9)

A pair of sharp shears are the most efficient way of cutting macrame cords. We emphasize the word sharp, because if the cut is unclean, the ends will fray. Choose a pair of shears that you find comfortable to work with— the larger the cord, the larger the shears should be. Conversely, fine cords and yarns can be cut with small sewing scissors.

DYES
(Plate 10)

Many materials such as jute, cable cord and sisal are only available in natural or, at best, a limited range of colors. For your project you may wish to use these cords in a wider range of colors to match or contrast with your clothing or room decor. Do not be afraid to dye your own. It is a simple process and can give very satisfactory results.

Before attempting to dye a specific cord, however, test-dye a small piece for color and shrinkage. To determine the degree of shrinkage (which will ultimately affect the length of cord you must cut for your project), cut a small piece, dye and thoroughly dry it, then compare it with the original length. Be careful, also, that the dye does not cause the cord to unravel, a problem common with sisal.

COMMERCIAL DYES
(Plate 10)

Most commercial dyes are easy to use and give very pleasing effects. Follow the manufacturer's instructions in preparing the dye bath. Remember that when a cord is freshly dyed it will probably be a shade darker when wet than when dry. Wind your cord into loose skeins for dyeing,

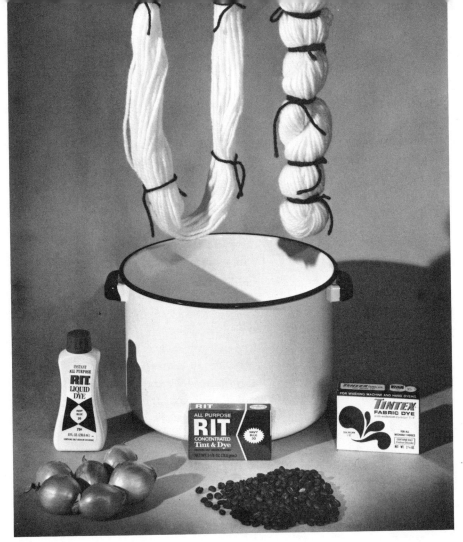

Plate 10. Try dyeing your own cords. The skein (left) has been tied for a uniform color dye. The other skein (right) has been tied for a variegated or tie-dyed effect.

allowing the dye to penetrate all the cords equally. To keep the cords from becoming tangled during the dyeing and drying processes, tie the skein at frequent intervals—tightly enough to hold the skein together but loose enough to allow the dye to penetrate the innermost cords.

If dyes out of a box or a bottle do not produce the exact shade you are looking for, experiment by mixing dye-solutions on your own.

CAUTION: Be sure to dye enough cord of a specific color to complete a given project. Matching colors by dyeing a second time is virtually impossible. Allow the dyed cords to hang freely and dry slowly at room

30

temperature. Do not use a tumble dryer to speed the drying process. It will tend to fade the color and may well demolish the cord structure and texture.

Natural Dyes
(Plate 10)

For a real adventure, you might wish to try dyeing cords the traditional way, using natural dyes. Until 1856, all fabric colors were produced in this way. The earliest recorded references to the use of natural dye-producing plants, flowers, roots and herbs is found in China around 3000 B.C.

Because of the great variation in colors produced by natural dyeing methods, manufacturers were only too happy to abandon natural dyes for the more predictable and reliable commercially produced chemicals. It is this lack of predictability, however, which has proven to be such an asset to the craftsman. Each dye lot and each dyeing process produces different colors, assuring the craftsman of one-of-a-kind results, often of subtle and interesting hue. Colors produced by natural dyes will vary depending on the season the material is collected, the moisture in the plant, the amount of sunlight it received and the nature of the soil in which the plant grew. During the dyeing process, color will also be affected by variation in measurements, temperature of the dye lots, length of time in the dye baths and the mineral and chemical content of the water being used.

It is for this reason that you should dye sufficient quantities at one time of each cord you intend using in a specific project. If matching is difficult with commercial dyes, it is virtually impossible using natural dyes.

Materials Required for Dyeing
(Plate 10)

Apart from the dyes themselves, only few materials are required. Soft water is almost essential, since the chemicals and minerals present in hard water will certainly affect the outcome in the dye bath. If natural, soft water is not available, commercial water softeners can be used. Use only enamel or copper pots. Pots made from other materials will affect the dye colors. The pots should be large enough for the entire quantity of cord to be completely submerged without crowding or bunching. Large containers, such as pails, will also be required to rinse the cords once they have been dyed. Use splinter-free sticks or heavy glass rods to stir the cords in the dyeing solution. You should also have a stove or other heat source to maintain a regulated temperature, and a thermometer to ensure the correct temperatures for the required length of time. During the dyeing process, it is advisable to wear long rubber gloves to keep your hands and arms from being stained with the dyes.

While the dyes themselves are natural, you will have to add certain chemicals called mordants, which prepare the cords to receive and combine with the dye to give the colors permanency. Mordants may be used prior to, during and after dyeing.

Alum, blue vitriol, chrome, copperas, tannic acid and tin are commonly used mordants, each being used for, and enhancing, a specific color. Frequently, Glauber's Salts are added to the dye bath, eliminating the need for constant stirring of the cords and producing a more even and uniform dye. Specific procedures and recipes will be found in the many good texts on the subject of natural dyes made at home.

Listed below are some of the colors, and the materials from which they can be obtained, to make natural dye:

REDS AND PINKS—Bloodroot, Cochineal, Crab Apples, Lavender and Rosemary extract, Madder, Pokeweed Berries, Scarlet Sage Blossoms, Tea Leaves.

BLUES—Indigo, Alkanet Roots, Elderberries, Logwood.

YELLOWS, GOLDS, BRASSES—Aster flowers, Tree Bark, Broomsedge, Yellow Camomile flowers, Coffee Beans, Cotton flowers, Goldenrod flowers, Lily-of-the-Valley leaves, Marigold flowers, Mountain-Laurel leaves, Onion skins, Osage Orange, Persian Berries, Poplar leaves, Privet leaves, Sumac berries, Sunflowers, Tulip Tree leaves, Zinnia flowers, Butterfly Weed blossoms, Chrysanthemum blossoms, Cockleburs, Dandelion blossoms, Day Lily blossoms, Mullein, Peach leaves, Queen Anne's Lace, Safflower, Sedge, Turmeric.

ORANGES—Coreopsis flowers, Dahlia flowers, Madder, Annatto, Cutch, Henna, Hollyhock blossoms, Lily-of-the-Valley leaves, Madder, Pokeweed berries, Safflower.

GREENS—Barberry plants, Burley Tobacco, Cockleburs, Floribunda Roses, Fustic, Goldenrod blossoms, Cutch, Indigo, Lily-of-the-Valley leaves, Privet, Seaweed, Sedge, Sumac, Sunflower seeds, Turmeric.

LAVENDERS AND PURPLES—Alkanet root, Blackberries, Cochineal, Concord Grapes, Cudbear, Elderberries, Logwood, Mulberries, Wild Grapes.

TANS AND BROWNS—Tree bark, Butternut hulls, Cutch, Pecan Hulls, Sassafras Root Bark, Walnut hulls, Acorns, Alkanet root, Barberry plant, Beets,

Blackberry vines, Bloodroot, Coffee, Pokeweed berries, Floribunda Rose plants, Hickory twigs, Privet clippings, Queen Anne's Lace, Cedar twigs, Onion skins, Safflower, Seaweed, Sedge, Sunflower seeds, Tea, Terra-Cotta clay, Tomato vines.

GRAYS AND BLACKS—Logwood, Barberry plants, Walnut hulls, Cochineal, Elderberries, Cutch, Multiflora Roses, Pecan Hulls, Seaweed, Sumac berries, Sunflower seeds, Wood Charcoal.

TIE-DYEING
(Plate 10)

Interesting effects may be achieved by tie-dyeing cords before beginning a macrame project. This process may be used with both commercial and natural dyes. Beginning with a light or white cord, tie it into a skein. The cords holding the skein together should be tied very tightly. One this is done, the skein may be folded in half and again tied tightly in several places. The reason for the tightly tied cords is to prevent your dye solution from completely penetrating all parts of the cords. After dyeing is completed, remove all the ties. Resecure your skein, but this time *loosely* and rinse thoroughly in cold water. You may repeat this process as often as you like using different colors, until the multi-colored effect of the cord is to your liking.

CLEANING PROJECTS

The method of cleaning will depend on the fiber content of the cord itself and any lining or decorative accessories which are included.

Cotton cords, sisal and various yarns may be washed. It is best to use cold water and one of the milder detergents made for cold water washing. Before washing however, check for shrinkage and colorfastness. Most cords will dry-clean satisfactorily. If in doubt check the fiber content of the cord and consult a reputable cleaner.

DETERMINING LENGTHS OF CORDS
(Plate 11)

There is no general rule to determine the amount of cord required for a specific project. It will vary from project to project due to several factors: the diameter of the cord, the number and sequence of knots, and the tension placed on the cords. The only accurate way of determining the amount of cord you'll need is to knot a sampler. Measure off a specific length of cord. Knot a small sample, using the same knots and pattern that you expect to use in the planned project. Measure the length of the knotted portion and the amount of cord it took to complete the sample. By dividing the length of the sample piece into the length of the completed project, you should get a very accurate idea of the amount of cord required. *For example:* You want to make a 36-inch belt. You find that to complete 6 inches of sample knots, it requires 1 yard of cord. Simply divide 6 into 36 and multiply the result by the 1 yard it took to make the sample. You would then be fairly safe in calculating that your 36 inch belt would require about 6 yards of cord to complete.

Plate 11. To knot a sample, measure the amount of cord accurately and knot a portion, using the same knot sequence as will go in the finished project.

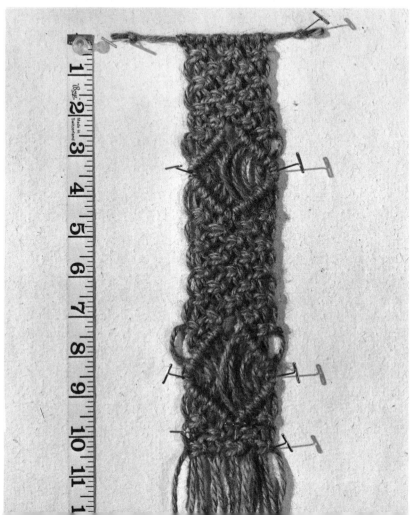

34

SUBSTITUTION OF CORDS

A variety of cords have been chosen for projects in this book. The pictures and the following descriptions will assist the reader to visualize some of the particular properties of the different cords, such as size, texture and sheen. If a specific type of cord is not available or a different texture is desired, feel free to substitute another material for the one specified. Your choice for an alternate cord should, however, be governed by the following principles:

First: The diameter of the cord should be approximately the same as the one suggested. Any drastic difference in size will alter the size of your knots and the overall length of your project.

Second: Your substitute cord should possess about the same tying properties as the original cord or as in the first principle, the overall size and texture of your project will be altered.

Third: Consider the ultimate purpose of your project. If the finished piece is to be subjected to considerable wear and tear, substituting a fragile cord for a more durable one would not be advisable.

Remember that each cord has its own properties when knotted. Before beginning a major project, therefore, it is always wise to test-knot a small piece of the cord you intend using. This will alert you to the properties of the cord and give you some idea how the knot pattern will look.

TYPES OF CORDS
(Plate 12)

Basically, anything which can be tied can be used for macrame. However, certain cords lend themselves more readily to macrame projects than others.

JUTE

Jute is one of the most inexpensive, readily available and easy to use knotting materials. It is strong and may be used many times over for practicing. Because it is inexpensive, it is an ideal material to use for learning. It also accepts dye admirably well, and because of its strong fibers, it is exceptionally long wearing. Lily produces a pre-dyed jute especially for macrame. It is available in 20 colors, in 4-ounce lots, each containing about 75 yards.

CABLE CORD

Most hardware or variety stores carry cable cord for tying packages. It is available in various diameters which depend on the number of strands of cotton in each cord. Cable cord also accepts dye very satisfactorily. Care must be taken, however, since cable cord has a tendency to unravel rather easily as the knots are being tied. To prevent this, tie the cut cord ends with a Simple Overhand Knot immediately after cutting. The cord ends may also be protected by wrapping them in tape.

Although cable cord will wear well and has good strength, because of its distinct texture and twist, many small knots tend to become obscured. If it is important to the overall pattern that each knot be visible, you should avoid using cable cord.

NYLON SEINE TWINE

The size range in nylon seine twine is almost limitless. It has a high gloss and creates a dramatic effect in macrame knotting. Like cable cord, it has a tendency to unravel when cut. To prevent this, you may either knot the ends with a Simple Overhand Knot as with cable cord or you may fuse the ends with an open flame. Before applying the flame however, test a small portion of the cord for flammability. Cut an inch off the cord, place it in an ashtray or other fireproof receptacle. Carefully hold a match to a tiny sample of the cord and if it bursts into flame avoid using this material.

Because of this cord's slippery texture, it may take considerable patience and practice to develop a suitable knotting technique.

SISAL

Cords made from this natural fiber, range in size from less than ⅛-inch to large ropes several inches in diameter. For the purpose of macrame, you should restrict yourself to sisal no larger than ¼-inch in diameter. While this material is very stiff and hard on the hands, it may be used for many effective projects. It is especially suitable for patio or other outdoor hangings. Weathering will only serve to enhance the natural beauty of its texture.

Sisal dyes readily, and many bright and attractive colors may be achieved. Before beginning a project using sisal, you will find it helpful to dampen the fibers to make them much softer and more pliable. However, check for shrinkage before wetting all your cord and make allowances where necessary.

CAUTION: Moisture tends to cause sisal to untwist, so, if possible, try to knot your entire project in one sitting, and eliminate having to wet your cords several times.

Plate 12. Many cords have been produced specifically for macrame, but almost anything that can be tied can be used. Cord sizes range from very fine yarn to heavy sisal and cable cord.

Yarns

Wool Rug Yarns are effective for many projects. They are available in a wide range of colors and textures and are soft and easy to work with. Unlike other wool yarns, rug wool has little elasticity, making the spacing of knots relatively easy. Yarns with too much elasticity make tension control and shaping much more difficult.

Cotton Yarns, commonly used in crochet work, weaving or tufting will give very interesting results. They have the added advantage of being available in a wide range of washable colors. Thicknesses range from the very fine, such as mercerized crochet cotton, to the much heavier rug yarns. They usually have little or no elasticity. Projects which require a soft absorbent fiber would be better if worked with cotton yarns.

Knitting Yarns may be used, but with extreme care. Because they have great elasticity, developing a suitable knotting technique can be very difficult. They have the advantage, however, of being available in a wide variety of colors. If bulk is desired, you may combine several strands for each knotting cord.

Rattail

One of the most attractive and easily knotted materials is known as rattail. It is a rayon-covered cotton cord measuring less than $1/8$-inch in diameter. It is usually available on spools or in skeins. The color range is broad. Because of its tight, highly polished surface, colors tend to be almost luminescent.

Rayon Cord

Another popular and attractive cord is a rayon-covered cotton cord with a diameter of approximately 3/16-inch. Unlike rattail, the weave of rayon is distinctly visible, resulting in less of a surface shine. Colors, as with rattail, are somewhat luminescent and their range is good. It is available in spools or skeins.

Polypropylene Cord

Several brands of polypropylene cord have been dyed and packaged especially for macrame. In most cases, the color range is limited. It is usually sold in small skeins, approximately 50 feet in length. Most

38

manufacturers specify that polypropylene is both colorfast and washable. This would make it especially suitable for outdoor projects. Because of its fiber characteristics, like nylon seine twine, its cut ends may be fused with flame, however, always test for flammability before selecting for a full project.

There are many other synthetic and natural fiber cords available. By all means experiment with new materials even if they are not mentioned in this book. However, before using an untried cord for a whole project, always test it for knotting characteristics, flammability and suitability of purpose, to avoid disappointment. The ingenuity and imagination is up to you.

2

Basic Cords, Knots and Patterns

This chapter introduces you to some of the basic uses of cords, and the knots and knotting patterns used in macrame. Rather than attempt to include all of the variations possible, some practical and decorative knots and patterns have been selected for use in the projects in this book. While many of the knots have several names, the most popular name has been used throughout the book in order to reduce confusion. Before beginning a specific project, prepare yourself with the necessary tools and a supply of an inexpensive, durable knotting cord, such as jute. Beginning with the Clove Hitch, master each of the knots and patterns involved to prepare yourself for a specific project later. Each knot has been assigned a symbol which will be used in the diagrams of the project section of the book as an aid to the written instructions. By becoming familiar with the knot symbols you will be able, by glancing at the project diagrams, to visualize the relationship of the various knots in a specific project. Frequently, basic knots are tied in such a manner as to produce often repeated patterns, such as a diamond, "X" or triangle. These patterns have also been included and diagramed in this chapter. Many knots may be tied from the left to the right, or from the right to the left. In multicolored projects it is advisable to tie knots from the left to the right on the left side of the project, and from the right to the left on the right side of the project. By doing this the colors will be balanced on both sides.

Fig. 1

HOLDING-CORD

(Fig. 1) The Holding-Cord is the dark, horizontal cord at the top with the pins at either end. Projects are usually begun on a holding-cord. The cord should be kept taut. In some projects the ends of the holding-cords are folded down beside the other cords and tied into the project itself.

CORE-CORD

(Fig. 2) The Core-Cord is the dark, vertical cord in the center. Knots are tied *around* the core-cord. The core-cord must be kept taut so that the knots may be tied around it. Knots will generally slide along the core-cord. One or more core-cords may be used for specific knots.

KNOTTING-CORD

(Fig. 2) The Knotting-Cord is the light-colored, knotted cord at the left. The knotting-cord is the cord with which knots are tied, usually around a core-cord or cords. One or more knotting-cords may be used for specific knots.

Fig. 2

SINNET

(Fig. 2) A Sinnet is a long string of knots. It usually consists of a series of one kind of knot, tied over one or more core-cords.

CLOVE HITCH

Knotting-cords are usually folded in half and mounted on a holding-cord or other device with the Clove Hitch.

(Fig. 3) Fold the knotting-cord in half and lay the fold over the holding-cord.

(Fig. 4) Bend the fold of the knotting-cord down behind the holding-cord to form a loop.

Fig. 3 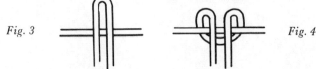 Fig. 4

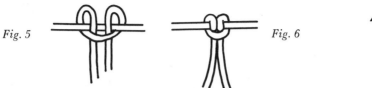

Fig. 5   Fig. 6

(Fig. 5) Tuck the 2 ends of the knotting-cord down through the loop.
(Fig. 6) Pull the 2 ends of the knotting-cord tight to form 1 Clove Hitch

OVERHAND KNOTS

The Overhand Knot is probably the most basic and widely known knot. It may be made with a single cord (the Simple Overhand Knot), with 2 cords (the Double Strand Overhand Knot), and with 3 or more cords (the Multiple-Strand Overhand Knot).

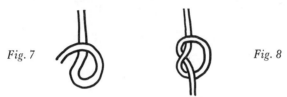

Fig. 7   Fig. 8

(Fig. 7) Begin the Simple Overhand Knot by forming a loop with the cord.
(Fig. 8) Carry the end of the cord through the loop and pull tight. This forms 1 Simple Overhand Knot.

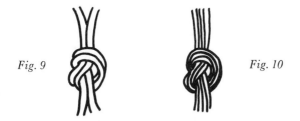

Fig. 9   Fig. 10

(Fig. 9) The Double Strand Overhand Knot is made in the same manner except 2 cords are used. The 2 cords should lay side-by-side and not become twisted.
(Fig. 10) The Multiple-Strand Overhand Knot is made with 3 or more cords. Try to prevent excessive twisting of the cords. Tie all the cords together, and then pull each cord separately to make the knot tight.

42

HALF KNOT

It will form a twisted sinnet. If the knot is tied from *left to right (fig. 11 and 12)*, the sinnet will twist in that direction. If the knot is tied from *right to left (fig. 13 and 14)*, the sinnet will twist in that direction. The knotting-cords travel around the core-cords with each successive knot causing the twist. To facilitate tying, pin the knots flat as you work to prevent the sinnet from twisting. The Half Knot may be tied over 1 or more core-cords, with 1 or more knotting-cords. The left cord becomes the *left knotting-cord*. The right cord becomes the *right knotting-cord*. The 2 center cords become the core-cords.

Fig. 11 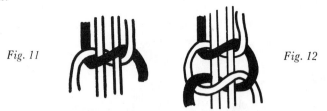 Fig. 12

(Fig. 11) Carry the left knotting-cord *over* the 2 core-cords and *under* the right knotting-cord. Carry the right knotting-cord *under* the 2 core-cords and *over* the left knotting-cord. This forms 1 Half Knot, right to left.
(Fig. 12) Carry the left knotting-cord *under* the 2 core-cords and *over* the right knotting-cord. Carry the right knotting-cord *over* the 2 core-cords and *under* the left knotting-cord. This forms the 2nd Half Knot, right to left. Repeat *fig. 11 and 12* for the required number of knots.

Fig. 13 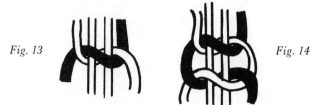 Fig. 14

(Fig. 13) Carry the right knotting-cord *over* the 2 core-cords and *under* the left knotting-cord. Carry the left knotting-cord *under* the 2 core-cords and *over* the right knotting-cord. This forms 1 Half Knot, left to right.
(Fig. 14) Carry the right knotting-cord *under* the 2 core-cords and *over* the left knotting-cord. Carry the left knotting-cord *over* the 2 core-cords and *under* the right knotting-cord. This forms the 2nd Half Knot, left to right. Repeat *fig. 13 and 14* for the required number of knots.

SQUARE KNOT

It is perhaps the most basic and widely used of all knots in macrame. Not only does it produce an attractive pattern by itself, but it is most effective in tying many cords together to produce a solidly knotted piece. The Square Knot may be tied over 1 or more core-cords with 1 or more knotting-cords. *(See figs. 23 through 26)*. Unlike the Half Knot, the knotting-cords do not travel around the core-cords, and consequently the knots do not twist. The knotting-cord which first crosses over the core-cord always remains on top of the core-cord. The left cord becomes the *left knotting-cord*. The right cord becomes the *right knotting-cord*. The 2 center cords become the core-cords.

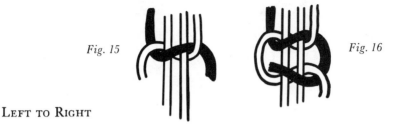

Fig. 15   *Fig. 16*

LEFT TO RIGHT

(Fig. 15) Carry the left knotting-cord *over* the 2 core-cords and *under* the right knotting-cord. Carry the right knotting-cord *under* the 2 core-cords and *over* the left knotting-cord.

(Fig. 16) Carry the right knotting-cord *under* the 2 core-cords and *over* the left knotting-cord. Carry the left knotting-cord *over* the 2 core-cords.

Fig. 17   *Fig. 18*

(Fig. 17) Carry the left knotting-cord *under* the right knotting-cord. This forms 1 Square Knot, left to right.

(Fig. 18) This figure represents 2 complete Square Knots, left to right. Repeat *figs. 15, 16 and 17* for the required number of knots.

Fig. 19   *Fig. 20*

RIGHT TO LEFT

(Fig. 19) Carry the right knotting-cord *over* the 2 core-cords and *under* the left knotting-cord. Carry the left knotting-cord *under* the 2 core-cords and *over* the right knotting-cord.

(Fig. 20) Carry the left knotting-cord *under* the 2 core-cords and *over* the right knotting-cords. Carry the right knotting-cord *over* the 2 core-cords.

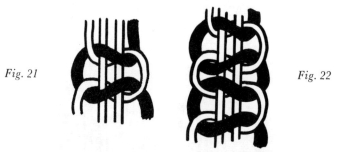

Fig. 21   *Fig. 22*

(Fig. 21) Carry the right knotting-cord *under* the left knotting-cord. This forms 1 Square Knot, right to left.

(Fig. 22) This figure represents 2 complete Square Knots, right to left. Repeat *fig. 19, 20 and 21,* for the required number of knots.

SQUARE KNOT WITH MULTIPLE CORDS

The Square Knot may be tied with any number of knotting-cords and core-cords. In this instance, 2 left and 2 right knotting-cords are tied around 4 core-cords. When tying with multiple cords, keep the cords flat, side-by-side. If the cords become twisted, the pattern becomes obscured. The knot may be tied from left to right, as in this diagram, or from right to left *(See fig. 19 through 22).*

(Fig. 23) Carry the 2 left knotting-cords *over* the 4 core-cords and *under* the 2 right knotting-cords.

(Fig. 24) Carry the 2 right knotting-cords *under* the 4 core-cords and *over* the 2 left knotting-cords.

Fig. 23   *Fig. 24*

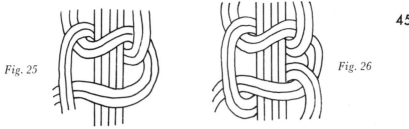

Fig. 25

Fig. 26

45

(*Fig. 25*) Carry the 2 left knotting-cords *over* the 4 core-cords and *under* the 2 right knotting-cords.

(*Fig. 26*) Carry the 2 right knotting-cords *under* the 4 core-cords and *over* the 2 left knotting-cords.

HALF HITCH

It will form a twisted sinnet. If the knot is tied from *left to right* (*fig. 27, 28 and 29*), the sinnet will twist in that direction. If the knot is tied from *right to left* (*fig. 30*), the sinnet will twist in that direction. The knotting-cord travels *around* the core-cord with each successive knot causing the twist. To facilitate tying, pin the knots flat as you work to prevent them from twisting. The Half Hitch may be tied over 1 or more core-cords, with 1 or more knotting-cords.

(*Fig. 27*) Carry the knotting-cord over the core-cord from left to right.

(*Fig. 28*) Carry the knotting-cord back under the core-cord and cross it over itself on the left side. This forms 1 Half Hitch, left to right.

Fig. 27

Fig. 28

(*Fig. 29*) Repeat *fig. 27 and 28* for the required number of knots.

(*Fig. 30*) To tie a Half Hitch, right to left, carry the knotting-cord over the core-cord, from right to left. Carry the knotting-cord back under the core-cord and cross it over itself on the right side. This forms 1 Half Hitch, right to left.

Fig. 29

Fig. 30

ALTERNATING HALF HITCH

Alternating Half Hitches and Alternating Double Half Hitches may be tied over 1 or more core-cords, with 1 or more knotting-cords. When tied in this sequence, the Half Hitches will not form twisted sinnets, but will lay flat.

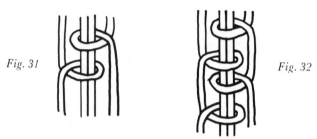

Fig. 31

Fig. 32

(Fig. 31) Tie 1 Half Hitch, right to left, followed by 1 Half Hitch, left to right.

(Fig. 32) Continue tying Half Hitches, in this sequence, for the required number of knots.

ALTERNATING DOUBLE HALF HITCH

(Fig. 33) Tie 2 Half Hitches, right to left, followed by 2 Half Hitches, left to right.

Fig. 33

Fig. 34

(Fig. 34) Continue tying Half Hitches in this sequence, for the required number of knots.

HORIZONTAL DOUBLE HALF HITCH

The horizontal cord becomes the core-cord. The vertical cords become the knotting-cords. A completed row of Horizontal Double Half Hitches will form a horizontal ridge of knots across the surface of the piece. This knot is usually tied with 1 knotting-cord over 1 or more core-cords.

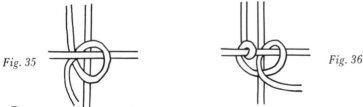

Fig. 35   Fig. 36

LEFT TO RIGHT

(Fig. 35) Carry the left knotting-cord around the core-cord, keeping the end of the cord on the left side of itself as it passes around the core-cord. *(Fig. 36)* Carry the knotting-cord around the core-cord a 2nd time on the right side of the 1st knot. Carry the end of the knotting-cord down through the loop. Pull the 2nd knot tight. This forms 1 Horizontal Double Half Hitch, left to right.

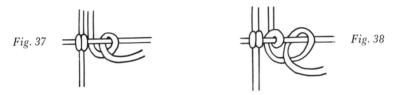

Fig. 37   Fig. 38

(Fig. 37) Repeat *fig. 35* with the 2nd knotting cord.
(Fig. 38) Repeat *fig. 36*. This forms the 2nd Horizontal Double Half Hitch, left to right. Repeat *fig. 35 and 36* for the required number of knots.

Fig. 39   Fig. 40

RIGHT TO LEFT

(Fig. 39) Carry the right knotting-cord around the core-cord, keeping the end of the cord on the right side of itself as it passes around the core-cord. *(Fig. 40)* Carry the knotting-cord around the core-cord a 2nd time on the left side of the 1st knot. Carry the end of the knotting-cord down through the loop. Pull the 2nd knot tight. This forms 1 Horizontal Double Half Hitch, right to left.

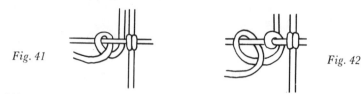

Fig. 41   Fig. 42

(Fig. 41) Repeat *fig. 39* with the 2nd knotting cord.
(Fig. 42) Repeat *fig. 40*. This forms the 2nd Horizontal Double Half Hitch, right to left. Repeat *fig. 39 and 40* for the required number of knots.

DIAGONAL DOUBLE HALF HITCH

The diagonal cord becomes the core-cord. The vertical cords become the knotting-cords. A completed row of Diagonal Double Half Hitches will form a diagonal ridge of knots across the surface of the piece. This knot is unsually tied with 1 knotting-cord over 1 or more core-cords.

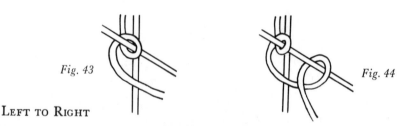

Fig. 43   Fig. 44

LEFT TO RIGHT

(Fig. 43) Carry the left knotting-cord around the core-cord, keeping the end of the cord on the left side of itself as it passes around the core-cord.
(Fig. 44) Carry the knotting-cord around the core-cord a 2nd time on the right side of the 1st knot. Carry the end of the knotting-cord down through the loop. Pull the 2nd knot tight. This forms 1 Diagonal Double Half Hitch, left to right.

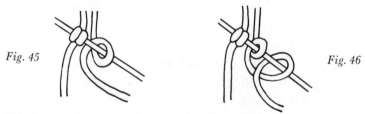

Fig. 45   Fig. 46

(Fig. 45) Repeat *fig. 43* with the 2nd knotting cord.
(Fig. 46) Repeat *fig. 44*. This forms the 2nd Diagonal Double Half Hitch, left to right. Repeat *fig. 43 and 44* for the required number of knots.

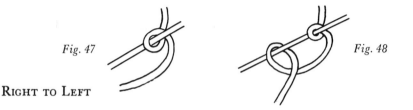

Fig. 47   Fig. 48

RIGHT TO LEFT

(Fig. 47) Carry the right knotting-cord around the core-cord, keeping the end of the cord on the right side of itself as it passes around the core-cord. *(Fig. 48)* Carry the knotting-cord around the core-cord a 2nd time on the left side of the 1st knot. Carry the end of the knotting-cord down through the loop. Pull the 2nd knot tight. This forms 1 Diagonal Double Half Hitch, right to left.

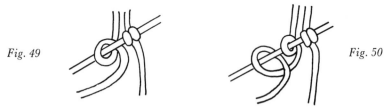

Fig. 49   Fig. 50

(Fig. 49) Repeat *fig. 47* with the 2nd knotting-cord.
(Fig. 50) Repeat *fig. 48.* This forms the 2nd Diagonal Double Half Hitch, right to left. Repeat *fig. 47 and 48* for the required number of knots.

VERTICAL DOUBLE HALF HITCH

The vertical cords become the core-cords. The horizontal cord becomes the knotting-cord. A completed row of Vertical Double Half Hitches will form a horizontal ridge of knots across the surface of the piece. This knot is usually tied with 1 knotting-cord over 1 or more core-cords.

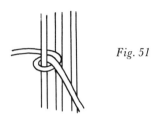

Fig. 51

LEFT TO RIGHT

(Fig. 51) Carry the knotting-cord around the left core-cord, keeping the end of the cord above itself as it passes around the core-cord.

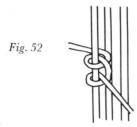

Fig. 52

(Fig. 52) Carry the knotting-cord around the left core-cord a 2nd time below the 1st knot. Carry the end of the knotting-cord through the loop. Pull the 2nd knot tight. This forms 1 Vertical Double Half Hitch, left to right.

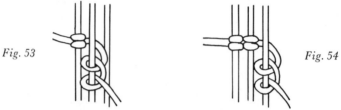

Fig. 53   *Fig. 54*

(Fig. 53) Repeat *fig. 51 and 52* on the 2nd core-cord. This forms the 2nd Vertical Double Half Hitch, left to right.

(Fig. 54) Repeat *fig. 51 and 52* for the required number of knots.

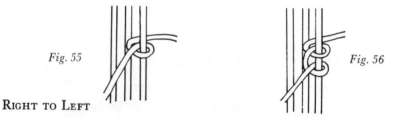

Fig. 55   *Fig. 56*

RIGHT TO LEFT

(Fig. 55) Carry the knotting-cord around the right core-cord, keeping the end of the cord above itself as it passes around the core-cord.

(Fig. 56) Carry the knotting-cord around the right core-cord a 2nd time below the 1st knot. Carry the end of the knotting-cord through the loop. Pull the 2nd knot tight. This forms 1 Vertical Double Half Hitch, right to left.

(Fig. 57) Repeat *fig. 55 and 56* on the 2nd core-cord. This forms the 2nd Vertical Double Half Hitch, right to left.

(Fig. 58) Repeat *fig. 55 and 56* for the required number of knots.

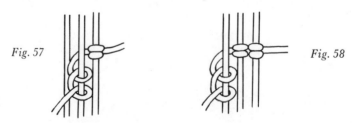

Fig. 57   *Fig. 58*

REVERSED DOUBLE HALF HITCH

This knot may be tied over 1 or more core-cords, with 1 or more knotting-cords. It may be tied from the left side *(fig. 59, 60 and 61)*, or from the right side *(fig. 62)*.

Fig. 59   Fig. 60

(Fig. 59) Tie 1 Half Hitch, left to right. Carry the knotting-cord under the core-cords.
(Fig. 60) Carry the knotting-cord back across the core-cords and pass it through the loop.

Fig. 61   Fig. 62

(Fig. 61) Repeat *fig. 59 and 60* for the required number of knots.
(Fig. 62) Tie 1 Half Hitch, right to left. Carry the knotting-cord under the core-cords. Carry the knotting-cord back across the core-cords and pass it through the loop. Repeat for the required number of knots.

ALTERNATING REVERSED DOUBLE HALF HITCH

This knot may be tied over 1 or more core-cords, with 1 or more knotting-cords.
(Fig. 63) Tie 1 Reversed Double Half Hitch from the right side. Tie 1 Reversed Double Half Hitch from the left side.
(Fig. 64) Repeat *fig. 63* for the required number of knots.

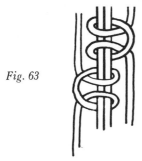

Fig. 63   Fig. 64

SINGLE CHAIN KNOT

This knot is actually a series of Alternating Half Hitches over *no core-cord*. The knotting-cord assumes the role of core-cord for each subsequent knot. This knot may only be tied with 2 cords.

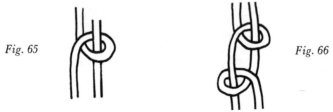

Fig. 65   *Fig. 66*

(*Fig. 65*) Hold the right cord taut. With the left cord, tie 1 Half Hitch, left to right over the right cord.

(*Fig. 66*) Hold the left cord taut. With the right cord, tie 1 Half Hitch, right to left over the left cord. Repeat *fig. 65 and 66* for the required number of knots.

DOUBLE CHAIN KNOT

This knot is actually a series of Single Chain Knots tied with 4 cords. The cords are divided into pairs. Each pair of knotting-cords assume the role of core-cords for each subsequent knot. This knot is usually tied with 4 cords.

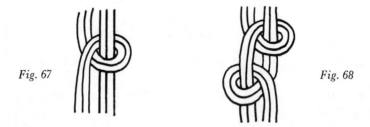

Fig. 67   *Fig. 68*

(*Fig. 67*) Hold the 2 right cords taut. With the 2 left cords, tie 1 Half Hitch, left to right, over the 2 right cords.

(*Fig. 68*) Hold the 2 left cords taut. With the 2 right cords, tie 1 Half Hitch, right to left, over the 2 left cords. Repeat *fig. 67 and 68* for the required number of knots.

ALTERNATING OVERHAND KNOTS

This knot may be tied on pairs of cords, or groups of cords divisible by 2, that is, 4, 6, 8, etc. In this case the knots have been tied on pairs of cords using the Double-Strand Overhand Knot. If the knots are tied on more cords, the Multiple-Strand Overhand Knot would be used.

Fig. 69   *Fig. 70*

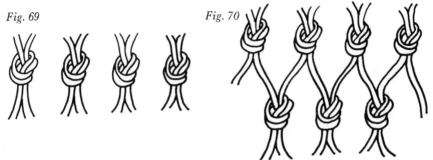

(Fig. 69) Divide the cords into pairs. Tie 1 Double-Strand Overhand Knot on each pair of cords, keeping the knots in a straight line.
(Fig. 70) Leaving the 1st cord on either side free, divide the balance of the cords into pairs. Tie 1 Double-Strand Overhand Knot on each pair of cords, keeping the knots in a straight line.

ALTERNATING SQUARE KNOTS

These knots consist of rows of Square Knots. The knots of each subsequent row alternate with the knots of the previous row. The 2nd row of knots is not tied with the same knotting-cords and core-cords as the 1st row. Rather, 1 knotting-cord and 1 core-cord from 1 knot, and 1 knotting-cord and 1 core-cord from its adjoining knot are tied together in a Square Knot.
(Fig. 71) Divide the cords into groups of 4. Tie 1 Square Knot on each group of 4 cords.
(Fig. 72) Leaving the first 2 cords on either side free, divide the balance of the cords into groups of 4. Tie 1 Square Knot on each group of 4 cords. Repeat *fig. 71 and 72* for the required number of rows. The 2nd and each succeeding row of knots are known as *Alternating Square Knots*.

Fig. 71   *Fig. 72*

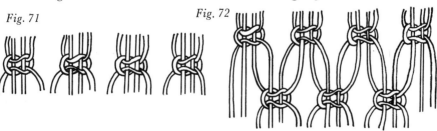

INTERLOCKING SQUARE KNOTS

These knots vary from Alternating Square Knots in that each subsequent row of knots is tied with the same knotting-cords over the same core-cord as the preceding row of knots. However, the adjoining knotting-cords are twisted around one another to tie the sinnets of Square Knots together.

Fig. 73

Fig. 74

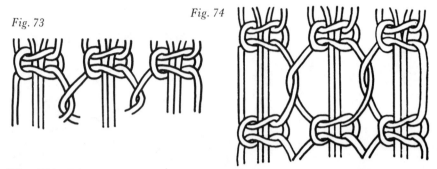

(*Fig. 73*) Divide the cords into groups of 4. Tie 1 Square Knot on each group of 4 cords. Wrap adjoining knotting-cords around one another.
(*Fig. 74*) Keeping the same group of 4 cords as in *fig. 73*, tie 1 Square Knot on each group of 4 cords. Repeat *fig. 73 and 74* for the required number of rows.

ADDING CORDS WITH SQUARE KNOTS

Cords may be added to increase the width of a project by tying them into rows of Alternating Square Knots. When cords are added in this manner decorative loops are formed at the top of each cord. These loops may be left plain or beads may be strung on the top of each loop. Cords may be added to the right side, as shown, or to the left side.

Fig. 75

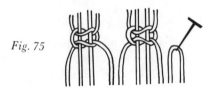

(*Fig. 75*) Fold 1 knotting-cord in half and pin the loop to the right of the last row of Alternating Square Knots.

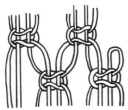

Fig. 76

(*Fig. 76*) Beginning with the 4 right cords, tie 1 row of Alternating Square Knots. If new cords are to be added repeat *fig. 75 and 76* for the required number of rows. If new cords are not to be added, continue tying the knots specified in the given project. If cords are to be added to the left, pin the knotting-cord to the left of the last row of Alternating Square Knots. Begin knotting the row of Alternating Square Knots from the left.

DIAMOND PATTERN OF DIAGONAL DOUBLE HALF HITCHES

The 2 center cords become the *left* and *right core-cords*. The other 4 cords on the left become the *left knotting-cords*. The other 4 cords on the right become the *right knotting-cords*.

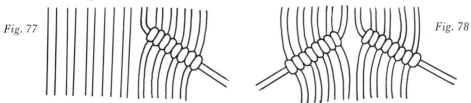

Fig. 77   Fig. 78

(*Fig. 77*) Carry the right core-cord diagonally across the right knotting-cords. Tie the right knotting-cords around the right core-cord with Diagonal Double Half Hitches.

(*Fig. 78*) Carry the left core-cord diagonally across the left knotting-cords. Tie the left knotting-cords around the left core-cord with Diagonal Double Half Hitches.

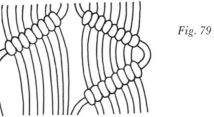

Fig. 79

(*Fig. 79*) Carry the right core-cord diagonally back to the center across the right knotting-cords. Tie the right knotting-cords around the right core-cord with Diagonal Double Half Hitches.

56

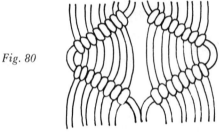

Fig. 80

(*Fig. 80*) Carry the left core-cord diagonally back to the center across the left knotting-cords. Tie the left knotting-cords around the left core-cord with Diagonal Double Half Hitches.

"X" PATTERN OF DIAGONAL DOUBLE HALF HITCHES

Divide the number of cords in half. The outside left cord becomes the *left core-cord*. The other 4 cords on the left become the *left knotting-cords*. The outside right cord becomes the *right core-cord*. The other 4 cords on the right become the *right knotting-cords*.

Fig. 81

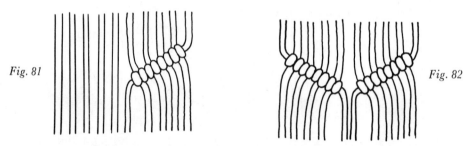

Fig. 82

(*Fig. 81*) Carry the right core-cord diagonally across the right knotting-cords. Tie the right knotting-cords around the right core-cord with Diagonal Double Half Hitches.

(*Fig. 82*) Carry the left core-cord diagonally across the left knotting-cords. Tie the left knotting-cords around the left core-cord with Diagonal Double Half Hitches.

Fig. 83

(*Fig. 83*) Cross the left core-cord over the right core-cord and carry it diagonally over the right knotting-cords. Tie the right knotting-cords around the left core-cord with Diagonal Double Half Hitches.

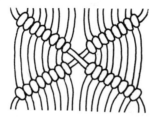

Fig. 84

(Fig. 84) Take the right core-cord, which lies under the left core-cord, and carry it diagonally *over* the left knotting-cords. Tie the left knotting cords around the right core-cord with Diagonal Double Half Hitches.

TRIANGLE PATTERN OF DIAGONAL DOUBLE HALF HITCHES

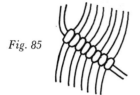

Fig. 85

Fig. 86

(Fig. 85) The left cord becomes the core-cord. Carry the core-cord diagonally across the 4 knotting-cords to its right. Tie the knotting-cords around the core-cord with Diagonal Double Half Hitches.

(Fig. 86) The left cord becomes the core-cord. Carry the core-cord diagonally across the 3 knotting-cords to its right. Do not include the core-cord from the previous row of knots. Tie the knotting-cords around the core-cord with Diagonal Double Half Hitches.

(Fig. 87) The left cord becomes the core-cord. Carry the core-cord diagonally across the 2 knotting-cords to its right. Do not include the core-cord from the previous row of knots. Tie the knotting-cords around the core-cord with Diagonal Double Half Hitches.

(Fig. 88) The left cord becomes the core-cord. Carry the core-cord diagonally across the 1 knotting-cord to its right. Do not include the core-cord from the previous row of knots. Tie the knotting-cord around the core-cord with 1 Diagonal Double Half Hitch.

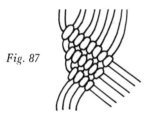

Fig. 87

Fig. 88

Below is a list of knots used in the various projects of the book together with the symbols assigned to each in the project diagrams.

Fig. 89

▼ CLOVE HITCH

♦ OVERHAND KNOTS

�–ᴍ HALF KNOT

■ SQUARE KNOT

■ SQUARE KNOT WITH MULTIPLE CORDS

◣ HALF HITCH

◣
◢ ALTERNATING HALF HITCH

◣
◣
◢
◢ ALTERNATING DOUBLE HALF HITCH

In the diagrams for the Horizontal, Diagonal and Vertical Double Half Hitches, the long solid line represents the core-cord and each short cross line represents 1 Double Half Hitch.

Fig. 90

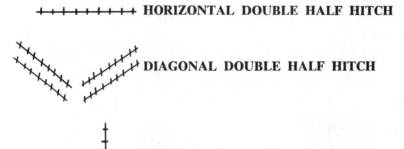

+++++++++ HORIZONTAL DOUBLE HALF HITCH

DIAGONAL DOUBLE HALF HITCH

VERTICAL DOUBLE HALF HITCH

 **REVERSED DOUBLE HALF HITCH**

 **ALTERNATING REVERSED DOUBLE HALF HITCH**

 **SINGLE CHAIN KNOT AND DOUBLE CHAIN KNOT**

 **ALTERNATING OVERHAND KNOT**

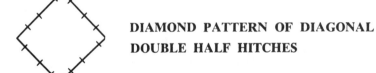 **ALTERNATING SQUARE KNOT**

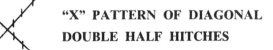 **INTERLOCKING SQUARE KNOT**

DIAMOND PATTERN OF DIAGONAL DOUBLE HALF HITCHES

"X" PATTERN OF DIAGONAL DOUBLE HALF HITCHES

TRIANGLE PATTERN OF DIAGONAL DOUBLE HALF HITCHES

3

Projects

If you have practiced the simple knots, you are now ready to choose a project.

Macrame items can be simply cord, knotted into a textile pattern—or the cord can be combined with beads, shells; or added as trim to suede belts, a fancy pillow or, perhaps, a purse you already have. We have included a great many projects to add interest to your wardrobe and excitement to various rooms in your home. Read all instructions carefully before you begin. If necessary, make a practice sample.

Perhaps you will be encouraged, as your skill increases, to adapt macrame to original projects of your own—possibly to replace a rush chair seat.

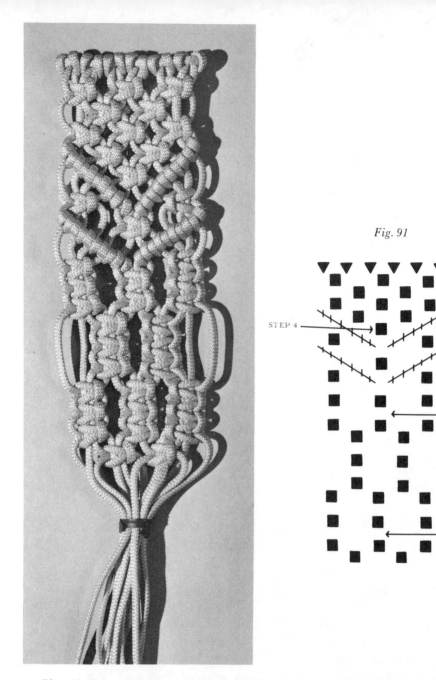

Fig. 91

STEP 1
STEP 2
STEP 3
STEP 5. 6. 7
STEP 4
STEP 8
STEP 9

STEP 10
STEP 11

STEP 12

STEP 13
STEP 14
STEP 15

Plate 13. *Before beginning a project, carefully study the knotting sample with its accompanying diagram and written instructions. By comparing the three, you will become familiar with the relationship of the knots, diagrams and written instructions.*

KNOTTING SAMPLE

(3¼″ by 8½″. See Fig. 91 and Plate 13)

MATERIALS

37′ rayon cord.

METHOD

Step 1. Cut 1 holding-cord 12″ long. Cut 6 knotting-cords, each 6′ long. Fold all the knotting-cords in half and mount them on the holding-cord with Clove Hitches.

Step 2. Beginning with the outside 4 cords on either side, tie 1 row of Square Knots.

Step 3. Tie 3 rows of Alternating Square Knots.

Step 4. With the 4 center cords, tie 1 Alternating Square Knot.

Step 5. Divide the number of cords in half. The outside left cord becomes the *left core-cord*. The other 5 cords on the left become the *left knotting-cords*. The outside right cord becomes the *right core-cord*. The other 5 cords on the right become the *right knotting-cords*.

Step 6. Carry the right core-cord diagonally across the right knotting-cords. Tie the right knotting-cords around the right core-cord with Diagonal Double Half Hitches.

Step 7. Carry the left core-cord diagonally across the left knotting-cords. Tie the left knotting-cords around the left core-cord with Diagonal Double Half Hitches.

Step 8. With the 4 left cords, tie 1 Square Knot. With the 4 right cords, tie 1 Square Knot. With the 4 center cords, tie 1 Square Knot.

Step 9. Repeat Steps 5, 6 and 7.

Step 10. With the 4 left cords, tie 3 Square Knots. Repeat this step on the right.

Step 11. With the 4 center cords, tie 2 Square Knots.

Step 12. With the 3rd, 4th, 5th and 6th cords from the left, tie 3 Square Knots. Repeat this step on the right.

Step 13. Repeat Step 10.

Step 14. With the 4 center cords, tie 3 Square Knots.

Step 15. With the 8 center cords, tie 2 Alternating Square Knots.

Fig. 92

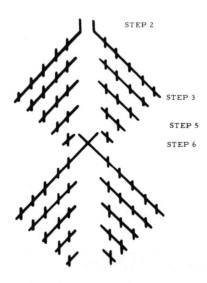

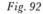

DOUBLE TRIANGLE BELT

(1" by 32", plus 12" ties at each end. See Fig. 92 and Plate 14)

MATERIALS

180′ nylon seine cord.

METHOD

Step 1. Cut 12 knotting-cords, each 15′ long. Arrange the cords on the knotting board side-by-side. Begin knotting 18″ from the point where the cords have been secured.

Step 2. The 2 center cords become the *left* and *right core-cords*. The other cords on the left become the *left knotting-cords*. The other cords on the right become the *right knotting-cords*.

Step 3. Carry the right core-cord diagonally across the right knotting-cords. Tie the right knotting-cords around the right core-cord with Diagonal Double Half Hitches.

Step 4. Carry the left core-cord diagonally across the left knotting-cords. Tie the left knotting-cords around the left core-cord with Diagonal Double Half Hitches.

Step 5. Repeat Steps 2, 3 and 4, four times. Do not include the core-cords from the preceding row of Diagonal Double Half Hitches in each subsequent row of knots.

Step 6. Twist the 2 center cords around one another, and repeat Steps 2 through 5. Continue until the desired length is reached. Trim all ends to 18″.

Step 7. Divide the cords at each end into pairs. Tie each pair of cords with Single Chain Knots. Tie 1 Double-Strand Overhand Knot at the end of the Single Chain Knots.

Plate 14. Double Triangle Belt (top). Diamond Pattern Belt (bottom). Nylon seine cord was used for these. Courtesy Evelyne Johnson.

Fig. 93

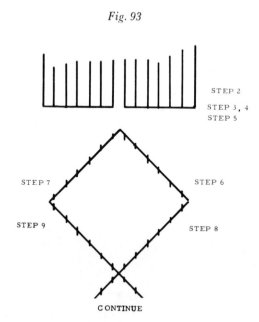

STEP 2

STEP 3, 4
STEP 5

STEP 7   STEP 6

STEP 9   STEP 8

CONTINUE

DIAMOND PATTERN BELT

(1¼" by 32", plus 12" ties at each end. See Fig. 93 and Plate 14)

MATERIALS

288′ nylon seine cord.

METHOD

Step 1. Cut 2 core-cords, each 24′ long. Cut 12 knotting-cords, each 15′ long. Arrange the cords on the knotting board with the core-cords on the outside. Begin knotting 18″ from the point where the cords have been secured.

Step 2. Divide the number of cords in half. The outside left cord becomes the *left core-cord*. The other 6 cords on the left become the *left knotting-cords*. The outside right cord becomes the *right core-cord*. The other 6 cords on the right become the *right knotting-cords*.

Step 3. Carry the right core-cord horizonally across the right knotting-cords. Tie the right knotting-cords around the right core-cord with Horizontal Double Half Hitches.

Step 4. Carry the left core-cord horizontally across the left knotting-cords. Tie the left knotting-cords around the left core-cord with Horizontal Double Half Hitches. Cross the right core-cord over the left core-cord.

Steps 5 through 9 will form a diamond pattern of Diagonal Double Half Hitches.

Step 5. The 2 center cords become the *left* and *right core-cords*. The other 6 cords on the left become the *left knotting-cords*. The other 6 cords on the right become the *right knotting-cords*.

Step 6. Carry the right core-cord diagonally across the right knotting-cords. Tie the right knotting-cords around the right core-cord with Diagonal Double Half Hitches.

Step 7. Carry the left core-cord diagonally across the left knotting-cords. Tie the left knotting-cords around the left core-cord with Diagonal Double Half Hitches.

Step 8. Carry the right core-cord diagonally back to the center across the right knotting-cords. Tie the right knotting cords around the right core-cords with Diagonal Double Half Hitches.

Step 9. Carry the left core-cord diagonally back to the center across the left knotting-cords. Tie the left knotting-cords around the left core-cord with Diagonal Double Half Hitches.

Step 10. Repeat Steps 5 through 9, adding 1 Multiple-Strand Square Knot in the center of every third diamond pattern. When the desired length has been reached, repeat Steps 2, 3 and 4. Trim all ends to 18".

Step 11. Divide the cords at each end into pairs. Tie each pair of cords with Single Chain Knots. Tie 1 Double-Strand Overhand Knot at the end of the Single Chain Knots.

Fig. 94

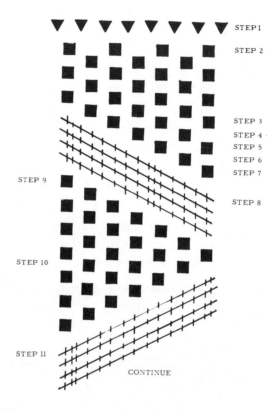

BANDED BELT

(2″ by 32″. See Fig. 94, Plate 15 and Color Plate XIII)

MATERIALS

60′ rose Lily Jute-tone; 60′ black rayon cord; belt buckle.

METHOD

Step 1. Cut 4 rose and 4 black knotting-cords, each 15′ long. Fold all the knotting-cords in half and mount them on the shank of the buckle with Clove Hitches in the following sequence: 2 rose, 4 black, 2 rose.

Step 2. Beginning with the outside 4 cords on either side, tie 1 row of Square Knots. Tie 5 rows of Alternating Square Knots.

Step 3. Beginning with the 4 right cords, tie 3 Alternating Square Knots.

Step 4. Leaving the 2 right cords free, tie 2 Alternating Square Knots below the knots tied in Step 3.

Step 5. Beginning with the 4 right cords, tie 2 Alternating Square Knots.

Step 6. Leaving the 2 right cords free, tie 1 Alternating Square Knot below the knots tied in Step 5.

Step 7. With the 4 right cords, tie 1 Alternating Square Knot.

Step 8. The outside left cord becomes the *core-cord*. The balance of the cords become knotting-cords. Carry the core-cord diagonally across the knotting-cords. Tie the knotting-cords around the core-cord with Diagonal Double Half Hitches. Repeat this step 3 times.

Step 9. Beginning with the 4 left cords, tie 7 rows of Alternating Square Knots.

Step 10. Tie 6 rows of Alternating Square Knots, decreasing each row by 1 Square Knot from the right side.

Step 11. The outside right cord becomes the core-cord. The balance of the cords become knotting-cords. Carry the core-cord diagonally across the knotting-cords. Tie the knotting-cords around the core-cord with Diagonal Double Half Hitches. Repeat this step 3 times.

Step 12. Repeat Step 9, beginning with the 4 *right* cords, instead of the 4 left cords.

Step 13. Tie 7 rows of Alternating Square Knots.

Step 14. Repeat Steps 11 and 12.

Step 15. Repeat Step 10, decreasing each row by 1 Square Knot from the *left* side, instead of from the right side.

Step 16. Repeat the above steps in the following sequence: 8, 9, 13, 15, 8, 9, 11, 12, 13. Carry all the cords to the reverse side and thread them through the back of several knots. Trim all the ends close to the back of the piece and glue in place.

Plate 15. Banded Belt. It combines a rough textured jute with a smooth textured rayon cord.

Fig. 95

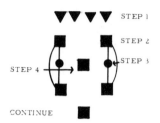

BEADED JUTE BELT

(1¾" by 38". See Fig. 95, Plate 16 and Color Plate XIII)

MATERIALS

60′ blue jute; 76 small beads; grommets; belt buckle.

METHOD

Step 1. Cut 4 knotting-cords, each 15′ long. Fold all the knotting-cords in half and mount them on the shank of the belt with Clove Hitches.

Step 2. Beginning with the outside 4 cords on either side, tie 2 Square Knots.

Step 3. String 1 bead on the 2nd cord from the outside, on both sides of the belt.

Step 4. With the 4 center cords, tie 1 Alternating Square Knot.

Step 5. Repeat Steps 2, 3 and 4 until the desired length is achieved. Carry all the cords to the reverse side and thread them through the back of several knots. Trim all the ends close to the back of the piece and glue in place. Set grommets between center Square Knots near the end of the belt to act as holes for the belt buckle tongue.

Plate 16. Beaded Belt. The basic Alternating Square Knot produces a handsome and durable pattern. The pattern has been enlivened with wooden beads and hand-dyed jute. Courtesy William Baker.

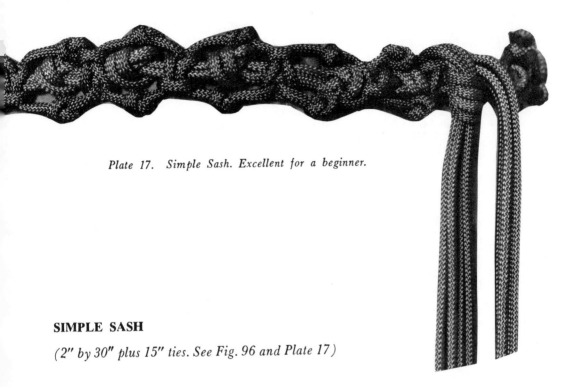

Plate 17. Simple Sash. Excellent for a beginner.

SIMPLE SASH

(2″ by 30″ plus 15″ ties. See Fig. 96 and Plate 17)

MATERIALS

    60′ heavy rayon cord.

METHOD

    Step 1. Cut 4 cords, each 15′ long. Tie all the cords together with 1 Square Knot 15″ from the point where the cords have been secured.

    Step 2. With the left cord, tie 1 Simple Overhand Knot. Repeat this step on the right.

    Step 3. With the 2 center cords, tie 1 Double-Strand Overhand Knot.

    Step 4. Tie 1 Square Knot.

    Step 5. Repeat Steps 2, 3 and 4 until the desired length is reached.

Fig. 96

STEP 1

STEP 2 ——◆ ◆ ◆—— STEP 2

STEP 3

STEP 4

CONTINUE

WIDE JUTE BELT

(2¾" by 37". See Fig. 97 Plate 18 and Color Plate XIII)

MATERIALS

96' rose jute; 54' natural jute; grommets; belt buckle.

METHOD

Step 1. Cut 4 rose and 2 natural knotting-cords, each 24' long. Fold all the knotting-cords in half and mount them on the shank of the buckle with Clove Hitches in the following sequence: 2 rose, 2 natural, 2 rose.

Step 2. Beginning with the outside 4 cords on either side, tie 1 row of Square Knots. Tie rows of Alternating Square Knots until the knotted portion measures 30".

Step 3. To narrow the belt so that it fits easily through the buckle, carry the 2 outside cords to the reverse side and thread them through the back of several knots. Trim the ends close to the back of the piece and glue down.

Fig. 97

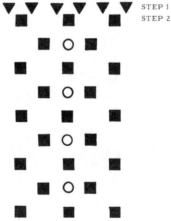

Step 4. With the remaining cords, continue tying rows of Alternating Square Knots for 7″. Carry all the cords to the reverse side and thread them through the back of several knots. Trim all the ends close to the back of the piece and glue in place.

Step 5. Set 1 grommet between each of the center Alternating Square Knots.

Step 6. Cut 4 natural cords, each 18″ long. Tie a 5″ sinnet of Square Knots. Wrap the sinnet around the belt 1″ to 2″ from the buckle to form a belt loop. Glue the ends to the back side of the belt.

Plate 18. Wide Jute Belt. Metal grommets are inserted between the center Square Knots. Dyed jute is at the outer edges, natural jute in the center. Courtesy William Baker.

CABLE CORD BELT

(1½" by 36". See Fig. 98 and Color Plate XIII)

MATERIALS

96' blue cable cord; 48' green cable cord; belt buckle.

METHOD

Step 1. Cut 4 blue and 2 green knotting-cords, each 24' long. Fold all the knotting-cords in half and mount them on the shank of the buckle with Clove Hitches in the following sequence: 2 blue, 2 green, 2 blue.

Step 2. Beginning with the outside 4 cords on either side, tie 1 row of Square Knots.

Step 3. With the 8 center cords, tie 2 Alternating Square Knots.

Step 4. With the 4 center cords, tie 1 Alternating Square Knot.

Steps 5 through 10 will form an "X" pattern of Diagonal Double Half Hitches and Square Knots.

Step 5. Divide the number of cords by half. The outside left cord becomes the *left core-cord*. The outside right cord becomes the *right core-cord*. The other 5 cords on the left become the *left knotting-cords*. The other 5 cords on the right become the *right knotting-cords*.

Step 6. Carry the right core-cord diagonally across the right knotting-cords. Tie the right knotting-cords around the right core-cord with Diagonal Double Half Hitches.

Step 7. Carry the left core-cord diagonally across the left knotting-cords. Tie the left knotting-cords around the left core-cord with Diagonal Double Half Hitches.

Step 8. With the 4 left cords, tie 1 Square Knot. Repeat this step on the right.

Step 9. Cross the left core-cord over the right core-cord and carry it diagonally over the right knotting-cords. Tie the right knotting-cords around the left core-cord with Diagonal Double Half Hitches.

Step 10. Take the right core-cord, which lies under the left core-cord, and carry it diagonally *over* the left knotting-cords. Tie the left knotting-cords around the right core-cord with Diagonal Double Half Hitches.

Step 11. With the 4 center cords, tie 1 Square Knot.

Step 12. With the 8 center cords, tie 2 Alternating Square Knots.

Step 13. Repeat Steps 2 through 12 until the desired length is achieved. Carry all the cords to the reverse side and thread them through the back of several knots. Trim all the ends close to the back of the piece and glue in place.

Fig. 98

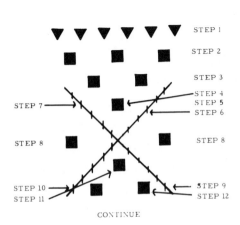

CONTINUE

LACY JUTE SASH

(2½" by 32", plus 16" tassels at each end. See Fig. 99 and Plate 19)

MATERIALS

180′ natural jute; 72 small beads.

METHOD

Step 1. Cut 12 knotting-cords, each 60″ long. Tie all the cords together with 1 Multiple-Strand Overhand Knot, 16″ from one end of the cords.

Step 2. With the 4 center cords, tie 1 Square Knot.

Step 3. With the 8 center cords, tie 2 Alternating Square Knots.

Step 4. Beginning with the outside 4 cords on either side, tie 1 row of Alternating Square Knots.

Step 5. Repeat Step 3, followed by Step 2.

Steps 6 through 10 will form a diamond pattern of Diagonal Double Half Hitches.

Step 6. The 2 center cords become the *left* and *right core-cords*. The other 5 cords on the left become the *left knotting-cords*. The other 5 cords on the right become the *right knotting-cords*.

Step 7. Carry the right core-cord diagonally across the right knotting cords. Tie the right knotting-cords around the right core-cord with Diagonal Double Half Hitches.

Step 8. Carry the left core-cord diagonally across the left knotting-cords. Tie the left knotting-cords around the left core-cord with Diagonal Double Half Hitches.

Step 9. Carry the right core-cord diagonally back to the center across the

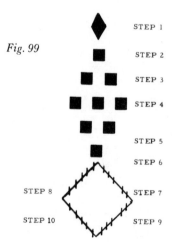

Fig. 99

STEP 1
STEP 2
STEP 3
STEP 4
STEP 5
STEP 6
STEP 8
STEP 7
STEP 10
STEP 9

right knotting-cords. Tie the right knotting-cords around the right core-cord with Diagonal Double Half Hitches.

Step 10. Carry the left core-cord diagonally back to the center across the left knotting-cords. Tie the left knotting-cords around the left core-cord with Diagonal Double Half Hitches.

Step 11. Repeat Steps 2 through 10, five times.

Step 12. Repeat Steps 2 through 5, one time.

Step 13. Tie all cords together with 1 Multiple-Strand Overhand Knot. String 3 beads on each cord. Tie 1 Simple Overhand Knot, on each cord, 12″ from the Multiple-Strand Overhand Knot. Trim all ends to 3″.

Plate 19. Lacy Jute Necklace (left). Lacy Jute Sash (right). A lightweight jute was loosely knotted to make a delicate, lacy pattern.

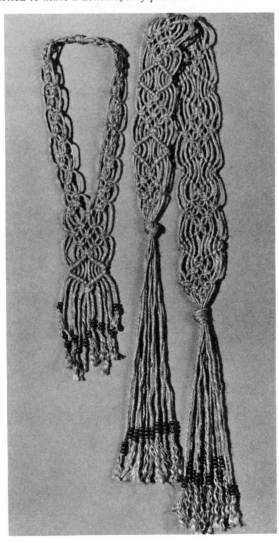

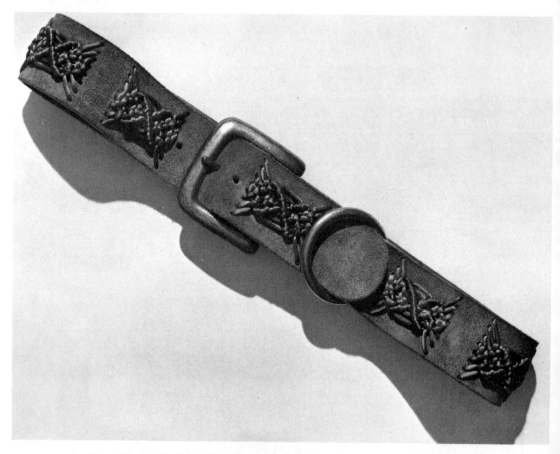

Plate 20. Suede Belt. This unusual project incorporates a shiny rayon cord knotted through a suede belt. Courtesy William Baker.

SUEDE BELT

(See Fig. 100 and Plate 20)

MATERIALS

Suede or leather belt 2″ wide by 37″ long; 48′ red rattail; 48′ blue rattail.

METHOD

Step 1. Cut a series of holes with a hole punch on the face of the belt. Holes should be slightly larger than the diameter of the rattail. For spacing, *see Fig. 100.* Cut 4 red and 4 blue cords, each 12′ long. Tie 1 Simple Overhand Knot at one end of each of the cords. Treat the other end of each cord with wax or glue to facilitate threading through the holes. Beginning at one end of the belt, thread the cords up through the holes in the belt in the following sequence: 2 red, 4 blue, 2 red. Leave the knots on the back of the belt.

Step 2. With the 4 center cords, tie 1 Square Knot. Tie 2 Alternating Square Knots. With the 4 center cords, tie 1 Alternating Square Knot. *Steps 3 through 7 will form an "X" pattern of Diagonal Double Half Hitches.*

Step 3. Divide the number of cords by half. The outside left cord becomes the *left knotting-cord.* The other 3 cords on the left become the *left knotting-cords.* The outside right cord becomes the *right core-cord.* The other 3 cords on the right become the *right knotting-cords.*

Fig. 100

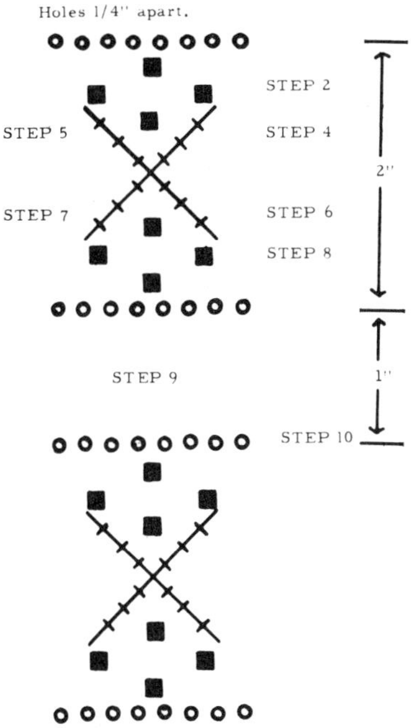

Step 4. Carry the right core-cord diagonally across the right knotting-cords. Tie the right knotting-cords around the right core-cord with Diagonal Double Half Hitches.

Step 5. Carry the left core-cord diagonally across the left knotting-cords. Tie the left knotting-cords around the left core-cord with Diagonal Double Half Hitches.

Step 6. Cross the left core-cord over the right core-cord and carry it diagonally over the right knotting-cords. Tie the right knotting-cords around the left core-cord with Diagonal Double Half Hitches.

Step 7. Take the right core-cord, which lies under the left core-cord, and carry is diagonally *over* the left knotting-cords. Tie the left knotting-cords around the right core-cord with Diagonal Double Half Hitches.

Step 8. Repeat Step 2.

Step 9. Thread the cords down through the 2nd row of holes. On the reverse side of the belt, reverse the color placement of the cords. That is, place the red cords in the center and the blue cords on the outside.

Step 10. Thread the cords up through the 3rd row of holes in the belt.

Step 11. Repeat Steps 2 through 10 for the entire length of the belt. At the last row of holes, tie 1 Simple Overhand Knot on the end of each cord close to the back of the belt. Trim the ends of the cord close to this knot.

Plate 21. Banded Sash. Bands of Double Half Hitches create varied widths. Courtesy Abbey Sperber.

BANDED SASH

(3" by 32", plus 30" ties on each end. See Fig. 101 and Plate 21)

MATERIALS

66′ brown cotton cord; 60′ orange cotton cord; 30′ gold cotton cord.

METHOD

Step 1. Cut 1 brown core-cord 21′ long. Cut 3 brown, 4 orange and 2 gold knotting-cords, each 15′ long. Arrange the cords, from the left, on the knotting board in the following sequence: 1 brown core-cord; 1 orange, 1 brown, 1 gold, 2 orange, 1 gold, 1 brown, 1 orange. Begin knotting 30″ from the point where the cords have been secured.

Step 2. Carry the core-cord horizontally across all the knotting cords. Tie all the knotting cords around the core-cord with Horizontal Double Half Hitches.

Step 3. With the 4 left cords, tie 1 Square Knot. Repeat this step on the right.

Step 4. With the 4 center cords, tie 2 Square Knots.

Step 5. Repeat Step 3, two times.

Step 6. Repeat Step 4, one time.

Step 7. Repeat Step 2, four times.

Step 8. Repeat Steps 4 and 5 two times. Repeat Step 4 one more time.

Step 9. Repeat Steps 7 and 8 until the desired length is achieved, as shown in Plate 21.

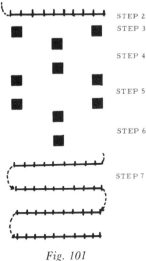

Fig. 101

"V" SASH

(2½" by 30, plus 22" ties on each end. See Fig. 102 and Plate 22)

MATERIALS

96′ blue cotton cord; 30′ white cotton cord; 30′ peach cotton cord.

METHOD

Step 1. Cut 1 blue core-cord 21′ long. Cut 5 blue, 2 white, and 2 peach knotting-cords, each 15′ long. Arrange the cords, from the left, on the knotting board in the following sequence: 1 blue core-cord; 2 blue, 1 white, 2 peach, 1 white, 3 blue.

Step 2. Begin knotting 22″ from the point where cords have been secured. Carry the core-cord diagonally across all the knotting-cords. Tie all the knotting-cords around the core-cord with Diagonal Double Half Hitches.

Step 3. With the 2 center cords, tie 3 Single Chain Knots. With the 2 left cords, tie 5 Single Chain Knots.

Step 4. Carry the core-cord diagonally back across all the knotting-cords. Tie all the knotting-cords around the core-cord with Diagonal Double Half Hitches.

Step 5. With the 2 center cords, tie 3 Single Chain Knots. With the 2 right cords, tie 5 Single Chain Knots.

Step 6. Repeat Steps 3 through 5 until the desired length is achieved.

Fig. 102

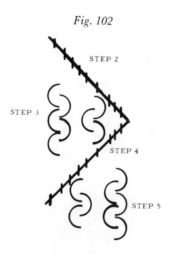

STEP 2

STEP 3

STEP 4

STEP 5

Plate 22. "V" Sash. Hand-dyed cotton cord and two simple knots make this simple but effective sash. Courtesy Abbey Sperber.

TRIPLE "V" SASH

(2½" by 32", plus 22" ties on each end. See Fig. 103 and Plate 23)

MATERIALS

96′ plum cotton cord; 30′ purple cotton cord; 30′ green cotton cord.

METHOD

Step 1. Cut 6 plum, 2 purple and 2 green knotting-cords, each 15′ long. Arrange the cords, from the left, on the knotting board in the following sequence: 2 plum, 1 purple, 2 green, 1 purple, 4 plum. Begin knotting 22″ from the point where the cords have been secured.

Step 2. The outside left cord becomes the core-cord. Carry the core-cord diagonally across all the knotting-cords. Tie all the knotting-cords around the core-cord with Diagonal Double Half Hitches. Repeat this step 1 more time.

Fig. 103

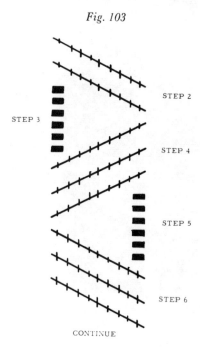

STEP 2

STEP 3

STEP 4

STEP 5

STEP 6

CONTINUE

Step 3. With the 4 left cords, tie 6 Half Knots.

Step 4. The outside right cord becomes the core-cord. Carry the core-cord diagonally across all the knotting-cords. Tie all the knotting-cords around the core-cord with Diagonal Double Half Hitches. Repeat this step 2 more times.

Step 5. With the 4 right cords, tie 6 Half Knots.

Step 6. Repeat Step 2, three times.

Step 7. Repeat Steps 3 through 6, until the desired length is reached.

Plate 23. Triple "V" Sash. It repeats several rows of Diagonal Double Half Hitches as an interesting variation of the "V" Sash (Plate 22). Courtesy Abbey Sperber.

CHEVRON SASH

(2" by 31", plus 15" ties on each end. See Fig. 104 and Plate 24)

MATERIALS

60′ green cotton cord; 60′ white cotton cord; 30′ peach cotton cord.

METHOD

Step 1. Cut 2 peach, 4 white and 4 green knotting-cords, each 15′ long. Arrange the cords on the knotting board in the following sequence: 1 peach; 1 white; 2 green, 2 white, 2 green, 1 white, 1 peach. Begin knotting 15″ from the point where cords have been secured.

Fig. 104

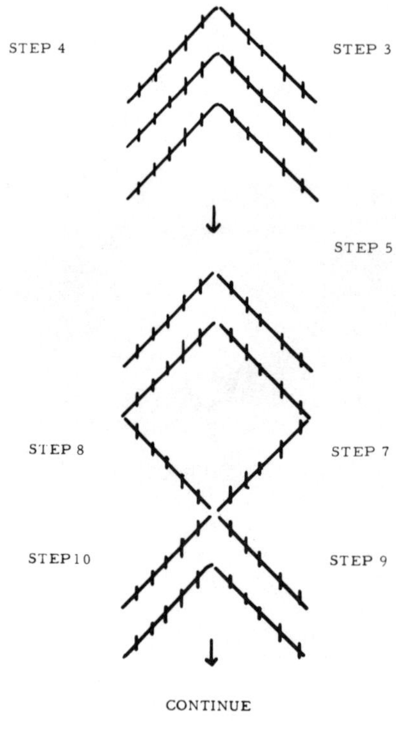

STEP 4   STEP 3

STEP 5

STEP 8   STEP 7

STEP 10   STEP 9

CONTINUE

Step 2. The 2 center cords become the *left* and *right core-cords*. The 4 cords on the left become the *left knotting-cords*. The other 4 cords on the right become the *right knotting-cords*.

Step 3. Carry the right core-cord diagonally across the right knotting-cords. Tie the right knotting-cords around the right core-cord with Diagonal Double Half Hitches.

Step 4. Carry the left core-cord diagonally across the left knotting-cords. Tie the left knotting-cords around the left core-cord with Diagonal Double Half Hitches.

Step 5. Repeat Steps 2, 3 and 4, thirteen times. Before beginning each subsequent row of Diagonal Double Half Hitches, cross the 2 center cords over one another. This will keep both sides of the sash joined.

Steps 6 through 10 will form an "X" pattern of Diagonal Double Half Hitches.

Step 6. Divide the number of cords in half. The outside left cord becomes the *left core-cord*. The other 4 cords on the left become the *left knotting-cords*. The outside right cord becomes the *right core-cord*. The other 4 cords on the right become the *right knotting-cords*.

Step 7. Carry the right core-cord diagonally across the right knotting-cords. Tie the right knotting-cords around the right core-cord with Diagonal Double Half Hitches.

Step 8. Carry the left core-cord diagonally across the left knotting-cords. Tie the left knotting-cords around the left core-cord with Diagonal Double Half Hitches.

Step 9. Cross the left core-cord over the right core-cord and carry it diagonally over the right knotting-cords. Tie the right knotting-cords around the left core-cord with Diagonal Double Half Hitches.

Step 10. Take the right core-cord, which lies under the left core-cord, and carry it diagonally *over* the left knotting-cords. Tie the left knotting-cords around the right core-cord with Diagonal Double Half Hitches.

Step 11. Repeat Steps 2 through 10, until the desired length is achieved.

Plate 24. Chevron Sash. Repeated rows of Diagonal Double Half Hitches produce a very heavy, solidly-knotted sash. Courtesy Abbey Sperber.

DIAMOND SASH

(2½" by 30", plus 22" ties on each end. See Fig. 105 and Plate 25)

MATERIALS

102′ green cotton cord; 30′ turquoise cotton cord; 30′ blue cotton cord.

METHOD

Step 1. Cut 2 green core-cords, each 21′ long. Cut 4 green, 2 turquoise and 2 blue knotting-cords, each 15′ long. Arrange the cords on the knotting board in the following sequence: 1 green core-cord, 2 green knotting-cords, 1 turquoise knotting-cord, 2 blue knotting-cords, 1 turquoise knotting-cord, 2 green knotting-cords, 1 green core-cord. Begin knotting 22″ from the point where cords have been secured.

Plate 25. Diamond Sash. The Diagonal Double Half Hitch will produce both diamond and "X" patterns, resulting in a light, delicate pattern. Courtesy Abbey Sperber.

Steps 2 through 6 will form an "X" pattern of Diagonal Double Half Hitches.

Step 2. Divide the number of cords in half. The outside left cord becomes the *left core-cord*. The other 4 cords on the left become the *left knotting-cords*. The outside right cord becomes the *right core-cord*. The other 4 cords on the right become the *right knotting-cords*.

Step 3. Carry the right core-cord diagonally across the right knotting-cords. Tie the right knotting-cords around the right core-cord with Diagonal Double Half Hitches.

Step 4. Carry the left core-cord diagonally across the left knotting-cords. Tie the left knotting-cords around the left core-cord with Diagonal Double Half Hitches.

Step 5. Cross the left core-cord over the right core-cord and carry it diagonally over the right knotting-cords. Tie the right knotting-cords around the left core-cord with Diagonal Double Half Hitches.

Step 6. Take the right core-cord, which lies under the left core-cord, and carry it diagonally *over* the left knotting-cords. Tie the left knotting-cords around the right core-cord with Diagonal Double Half Hitches.

Step 7. Repeat Steps 2 through 6, until the desired length is reached.

Fig. 105

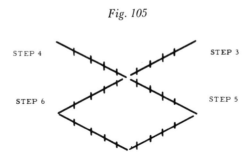

STEP 4   STEP 3

STEP 6   STEP 5

Plate 26. Radiating Bands Sash. By combining Diagonal and Horizontal Double Half Hitches, a star or radiating pattern of knots is achieved. Courtesy Abbey Sperber.

RADIATING BANDS SASH

(2½" by 32", plus 16" ties at each end. See Fig. 106 and Plate 26)

MATERIALS

    42′ blue cotton cord; 60′ orange cotton cord; 60′ purple cotton cord.

METHOD

Step 1. Cut 2 blue knotting-cords, each 21′ long. Cut 4 orange and 4 purple knotting-cords, each 15′ long. Arrange the cords on the knotting board in the following sequence: 2 purple, 2 orange, 2 blue, 2 orange, 2 purple. Begin knotting 16″ from the point where cords have been secured.

Step 2. The 2 center cords become the *left* and *right core-cords*. The 4 cords on the left become the *left knotting-cords*. The other 4 cords on the right become the *right knotting-cords*.

Step 3. Carry the right core-cord diagonally across the right knotting-cords. Tie the right knotting-cords around the right core-cord with Diagonal Double Half Hitches.

Step 4. Carry the left core-cord diagonally across the left knotting-cords. Tie the left knotting-cords around the left core-cord with Diagonal Double Half Hitches.

Step 5. Carry the right core-cord diagonally back to the center across the right knotting-cords. Tie the right knotting-cords around the right core-cord with Diagonal Double Half Hitches.

Step 6. Carry the left core-cord diagonally back to the center across the left knotting-cords. Tie the left knotting-cords around the left core-cord with Diagonal Double Half Hitches. Cross the left core-cord over the right core-cord.

Step 7. Divide the number of cords by half. The outside left cord becomes the *left core-cord*. The other 4 cords on the left become the *left knotting-cords*. The outside right cord becomes the *right core-cord*. The other 4 cords on the right become the *right knotting-cords*.

Step 8. Carry the right core-cord diagonally across the right knotting-cords. Tie the right knotting-cords around the right core-cord with Diagonal Double Half Hitches.

Step 9. Carry the left core-cord diagonally across the left knotting-cords. Tie the left knotting-cords around the left core-cord with Diagonal Double Half Hitches.

Step 10. Repeat Steps 2, 3 and 4, except carry the core-cord *horizontally* across the knotting-cords, and tie the knotting-cords with *Horizontal Double Half Hitches*. Repeat this Step, one more time.

Step 11. Repeat Steps 2, 3 and 4, two times.

Step 12. Repeat this pattern until the desired length is reached.

Fig. 106

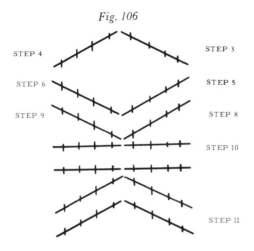

STEP 4   STEP 3

STEP 6   STEP 5

STEP 9   STEP 8

STEP 10

STEP 11

Plate 27. *Beaded Jute Sash. Hand-dyed jute and simple wooden beads combine to form a handsome masculine sash. Courtesy William Baker.*

BEADED JUTE SASH

(1½" by 58", plus 10" fringe. See Fig. 107, Plate 27 and Color Plate XIII)

MATERIALS

48′ green jute; 48′ blue jute; 24 large beads.

METHOD

Step 1. Cut 4 green and 4 blue knotting-cords, each 12′ long. Arrange the cords on the knotting board in the following sequence: 1 green, 1 blue, 1 green, 2 blue, 1 green, 1 blue, 1 green. Begin knotting 12″ from the point where the cords have been secured.

Step 2. With the 4 center cords, tie 1 Square Knot.

Step 3. Tie 6 rows of Alternating Square Knots.

Steps 4 through 9 will form an "X" pattern of Diagonal Double Half Hitches with 1 large bead on each side of the belt.

Step 4. Divide the number of cords in half. The outside left cord becomes the *left core-cord*. The outside right cord becomes the *right core-cord*. The other 3 cords on the left become the *left knotting-cords*. The other 3 cords on the right become the *right knotting-cords*.

Step 5. Carry the right core-cord diagonally across the right knotting-cords. Tie the right knotting-cords around the right core-cord with Diagonal Double Half Hitches.

Step 6. Carry the left core-cord diagonally across the left knotting-cords. Tie the left knotting-cords around the left core-cord with Diagonal Double Half Hitches.

Step 7. String 1 bead on the 2nd cord from the outside, on both sides of the belt.

Step 8. Cross the left core-cord over the right core-cord and carry it diagonally over the right knotting-cords. Tie the right knotting-cords around the left core-cord with Diagonal Double Half Hitches.

Step 9. Take the right core-cord, which lies under the left core-cord, and carry it diagonally *over* the left knotting-cords. Tie the left knotting-cords around the right core-cord with Diagonal Double Half Hitches.

Step 10. Repeat Steps 2 through 9, eleven times.

Step 11. Repeat Steps 2 and 3.

Step 12. Tie 1 Simple Overhand Knot on each cord next to each outside Square Knot. Tie 1 Simple Overhand Knot 1″ from the end of each cord.

Fig. 107

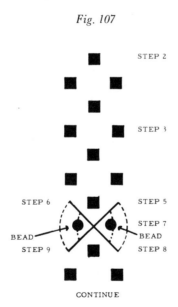

Plate 28. Triangle Choker. Nylon seine cord was used to produce a pearl-like effect. This is a companion piece to the Double Triangle Belt (Plate 14). Courtesy Evelyne Johnson.

TRIANGLE CHOKER

(½" by 8", plus 8" ties on each end. See Fig. 108 and Plate 28)

MATERIALS

24' nylon seine cord.

METHOD

Step 1. Cut 6 knotting-cords, each 4' long. Tie all the cords together with 1 Multiple-Strand Overhand Knot, 8" from the point where the cords have been secured.

Step 2. The outside left cord will be the *core-cord*. The other 5 cords will be the *knotting-cords*. Carry the core-cord diagonally across the knotting-cords. Tie the knotting-cords around the core-cord with Diagonal Double Half Hitches.

Step 3. Repeat Step 2, four times. Do not include the core-cord from the preceding row of Diagonal Double Half Hitches in each subsequent row of knots.

Step 4. Repeat Steps 2 and 3, until the desired length is reached. Tie all the cords together with 1 Multiple-Strand Overhand Knot after the last triangle pattern. Trim all ends to 8".

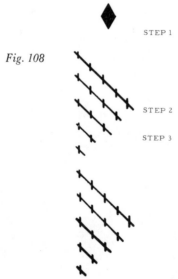

STEP 1

Fig. 108

STEP 2

STEP 3

ZIGZAG CHOKER

(See Fig. 109 and Plate 29)

MATERIALS

26′ nylon seine cord.

METHOD

Step 1. Cut 1 core-cord 6′ long. Cut 5 knotting-cords, each 4′ long. Arrange the cords on the knotting board with the core-cord on the left. Begin knotting 10″ from the point where the cords have been secured.

Step 2. Carry the core-cord diagonally across all the knotting-cords. Tie the knotting-cords around the core-cord with Diagonal Double Half Hitches.

Step 3. Carry the core-cord diagonally back across all the knotting-cords. Tie the knotting-cords around the core-cord with Diagonal Double Half Hitches.

Step 4. Repeat Steps 2 and 3, until the desired length is reached. Trim all ends to 10″.

Fig. 109

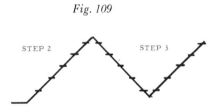

Plate 29. Zigzag Choker, with washable nylon seine cord. It's a companion to Diamond Pattern Belt (Plate 14). Courtesy Evelyne Johnson.

SIMPLE BEADED CHOKER

(See Fig. 110 and Plate 30)

MATERIALS

12′ cable cord; 20 small beads.

Plate 30. Ideal for the beginner.

METHOD

Step 1. Cut 1 core-cord 3′ long. Cut 2 knotting-cords, each 4½′ long. String 20 beads on the core-cord. Tie a Simple Overhand Knot at each end of all the cords. Arrange the cords on the knotting board with the core-cord in the center.

Step 2. Tie all the cords together with 1 Multiple-Strand Overhand Knot, 8″ from the point where the cords have been secured.

Step 3. Push 1 bead up against the Multiple-Strand Overhand Knot. With the left knotting cord, tie 1 Reversed Double Half Hitch, leaving ¾″ between the core-cord and the outside loop of the knot.

Step 4. Push 1 bead up against this knot. With the right knotting-cord, tie 1 Reversed Double Half Hitch, leaving ¾″ between the core-cord and the outside loop of the knot.

Step 5. Push 1 bead up against this knot. With the left knotting-cord, tie 1 Reversed Double Half Hitch, leaving ¾″ between the core-cord and the outside loop of the knot.

Step 6. Repeat Steps 4 and 5 until all the beads have been used. Tie all the cords together with 1 Multiple-Strand Overhand Knot. Trim the ends to 8″ and tie 1 Simple Overhand Knot at the end of each cord.

Fig. 110

STEP 2

STEP 3

STEP 4

STEP 5

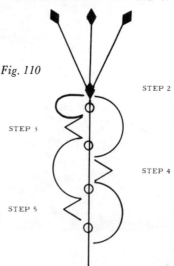

Plate I. Sisal Tote Bag (rear). Rayon Bag (left). Wool
Bag (right).

Plate II. Rayon Chevron Pillow Top (left). Braided
Pillow Top (center). Square Knot Pillow Top (right).
These tops were made with rayon cords and rug yarns.

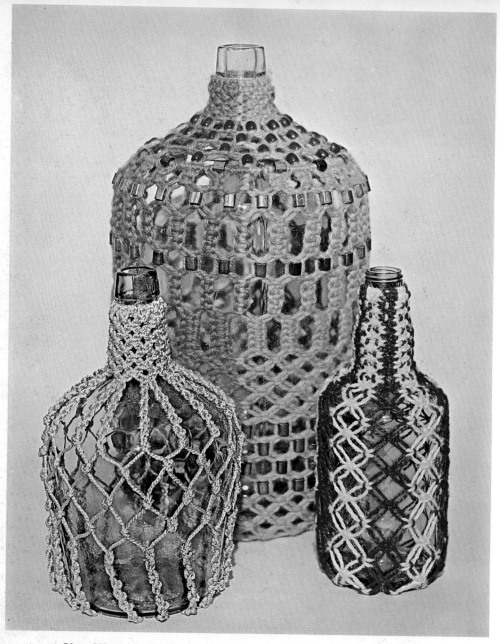

Plate III. Rayon Bottle Cover (left). Beaded Bottle Cover (center). Jute Bottle Cover (right). Unusual decorative accessories made from ordinary bottles whose shapes have been accented by decorative knot patterns, colorful cords, and accent beads.

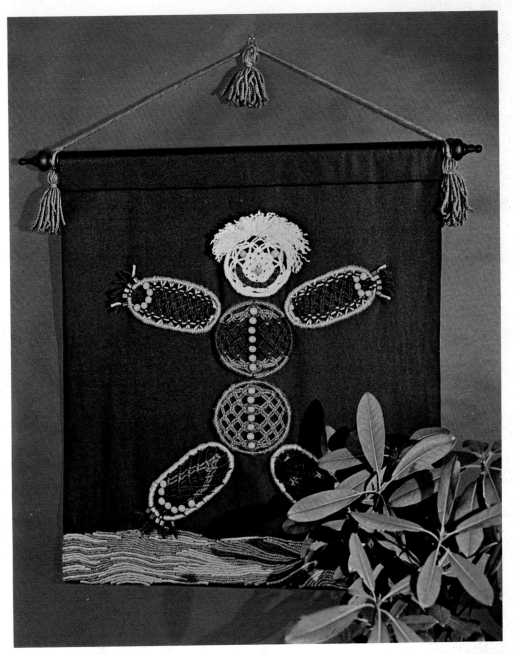

Plate IV. Scarecrow. A three-dimensional effect is achieved by using embroidery hoops to outline the sections of the body. The wild and wooly hair is made with rug yarn which has been untwisted.

Plate VI. Jute Wall Hanging. A long, slender wall hanging for those hard-to-decorate narrow areas. The free-flowing line of knots in the center of the hanging is particularly engaging. Courtesy Terry Schwartz.

Plate V. Christmas Tree. Three-dimensional tabletop Christmas Tree fashioned from two wall hangings, sewn together and placed over a wooden frame.

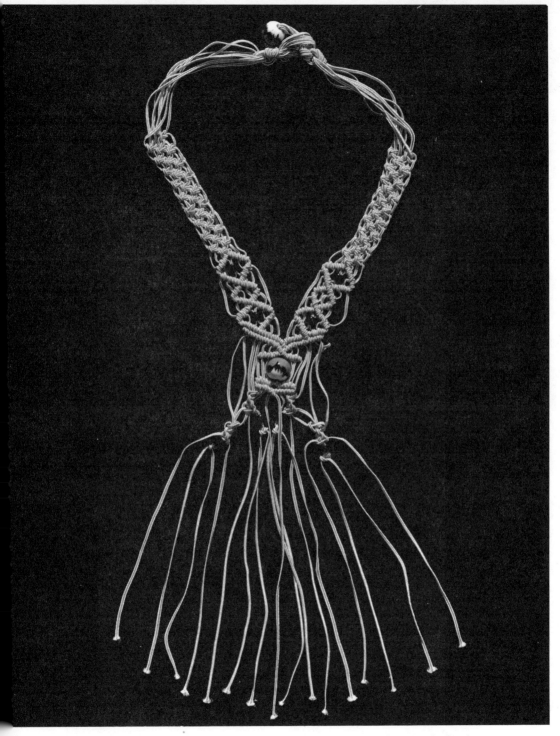

Plate 31. Rayon Necklace. Fine rayon cords and handmade ceramic beads combine for a sophisticated and unusual necklace. Courtesy Abbey Sperber.

98

BEADED RAYON NECKLACE

(See Fig. 111 and Plate 31)

MATERIALS

120′ thin pink rayon cord; 8 small beads; 2 large beads.

METHOD

Step 1. Cut 4 cords, each 15′ long. String 1 large bead on all 4 cords and center it. Fold the cords in half over the bead. Tie the 8 cords together, 1″ below the bead, with 3 Double Chain Knots using 4 cords for each side of the chain.

Step 2. Tie 2 Square Knots 4″ below the last Double Chain Knot. Tie 17 rows of Alternating Square Knots.

Steps 3 through 7 will form a Diamond Pattern of Diagonal Double Half Hitches.

Step 3. The 2 center cords become the *left* and *right core-cords*. The other 3 cords on the left become the *left knotting-cords*. The other 3 cords on the right become the *right knotting cords*.

Step 4. Carry the right core-cord diagonally across the right knotting-cords. Tie the right knotting-cords around the right core-cord with Diagonal Double Half Hitches.

Step 5. Carry the left core-cord diagonally across the left knotting-cords. Tie the left knotting-cords around the left core-cord with Diagonal Double Half Hitches. String 1 small bead on the 2 center cords.

Step 6. Carry the right core-cord diagonally back to the center across the right knotting-cords. Tie the right knotting-cords around the right core-cord with Diagonal Double Half Hitches.

Step 7. Carry the left core-cord diagonally back to the center across the left knotting-cords. Tie the left knotting-cords around the left core-cord with Diagonal Double Half Hitches.

Step 8. Repeat Steps 3 through 7, *except* the core-cords will cover only 2 knotting-cords on each side, and no bead is added in the center.

Step 9. Repeat Steps 3 through 7.

Step 10. Repeat Steps 1 through 9, except 1 large bead is not used in Step 1. A loop will be formed, through which the large bead may be buttoned.

Step 11. Lay the 2 knotted sides of the necklace together with the lowest diamond patterns side-by-side. This will be the center front of the necklace. Carry the core-cord which formed the bottom outside portion of the diamond patterns in Steps 3 through 7, across the 6 knotting-cords in the center (3 on the right and 3 on the left). Tie the 6 knotting-cords around the core-cords with Diagonal Double Half Hitches.

Step 12. Divide the number of cords in half. The outside left cord becomes the *left core-cord*. The other 7 cords on the left become the *left knotting-cords*. The outside right cord becomes the *right core-cord*. The other 7 cords on the right become the *right knotting-cords*.

Step 13. Carry the right core-cord diagonally across the right knotting-cords. Tie the right knotting-cords around the right core-cord with Diagonal Double Half Hitches.

Step 14. Carry the left core-cord diagonally across the left knotting-cords. Tie the left knotting-cords around the left core-cord with Diagonal Double Half Hitches.

Step 15. This step will join the both sides of the necklace together in the center-front. Cross the left core-cord (Step 12) over the right core-cord (Step 12) and carry it horizontally across the 3 right knotting-cords. Tie the 3 right knotting-cords around the left core-cord with Horizontal Double Half Hitches. Take the right core-cord, which lies under the left core-cord, and carry it horizontally *over* the 3 left knotting-cords. Tie the 3 left knotting-cords around the right core-cord with Horizontal Double Half Hitches.

Step 16. String 1 large bead on the 2 center cords. These center cords become the left and right core-cords. Carry the right core-cord horizontally across the 3 right knotting-cords. Tie the 3 right knotting-cords around the right core-cord with Horizontal Double Half Hitches. Carry the left core-cord horizontally across the 3 left knotting-cords. Tie the 3 left knotting-cords around the left core-cord with Horizontal Double Half Hitches.

Step 17. Carry the right core-cord horizontally back to the center across the 3 right knotting-cords. Tie the 3 right knotting-cords around the right core-cord with Horizontal Double Half Hitches. Carry the left core-cord horizontally back to the center across the 3 left knotting-cords. Tie the 3 left knotting-cords around the left core-cord with Horizontal Double Half Hitches.

Step 18. With the 4 center cords, tie 1 Square Knot.

Step 19. With the 3rd, 4th, 5th and 6th cords from the left, tie 5 Half Knots. With the 4 left cords, tie 5 Half Knots. String 1 small bead on the

2nd and 3rd cords from the left. String 1 small bead on the 6th and 7th cords from the left. Tie 2 Single Chain Knots below each small bead. Repeat this step on the right. Trim all ends to 7".

Fig. 111

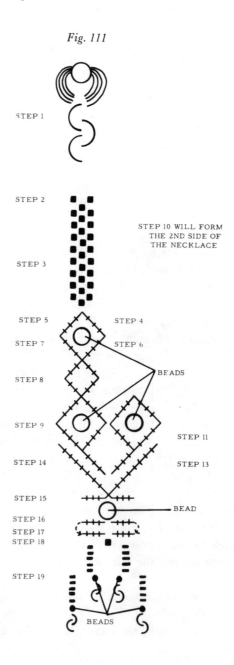

STEP 1

STEP 2

STEP 10 WILL FORM
THE 2ND SIDE OF
THE NECKLACE

STEP 3

STEP 5   STEP 4

STEP 7   STEP 6

BEADS

STEP 8

STEP 9

STEP 11

STEP 14   STEP 13

STEP 15   BEAD

STEP 16

STEP 17

STEP 18

STEP 19

BEADS

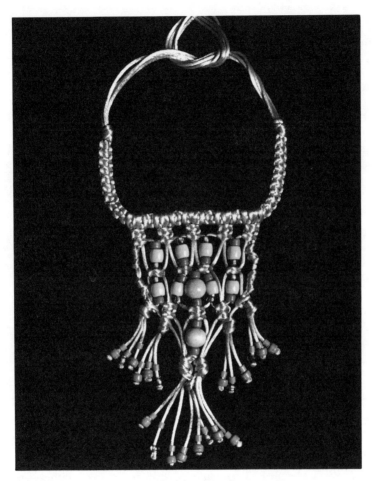

Plate 32. Party Necklace. An imaginative use of many different bead shapes and a brilliantly shiny rayon cord produce a dress-up necklace. Courtesy Esta-Gail Reisman.

PARTY NECKLACE

(See Fig. 112 and Plate 32)

MATERIALS

48′ gold rattail; 58 small beads; 8 barrel beads; 2 large beads.

METHOD

Step 1. Cut 4 cords, each 6′ long. Working from the center of these 4 cords, tie a sinnet of Square Knots with 18 Square Knots on both sides of the center. Tie 1 Multiple-Strand Overhand Knot at each end of the sinnet directly below the last Square Knot. Tie 1 Double-Strand Overhand Knot at the end of each pair of cords. This sinnet will be the holding cord for the necklace.

Step 2. Cut 10 cords, each 3′ long. Fold all the cords in half and mount them on the center of the holding-cord with Clove Hitches.

Step 3. Divide the cords into groups of 4. Tie 2 Square Knots on each group of 4 cords.

Step 4. With the 2 left cords, tie 4 Double-Strand Overhand Knots. Repeat this step on the right.

Step 5. The 4th, 5th, 8th and 9th cords from each side will be core-cords. String 1 small bead, 1 barrel bead, and 1 small bead on each pair of core-cords.

Step 6. Tie 1 Square Knot below the last small bead on each pair of core-cords.

Step 7. Repeat Step 5.

Step 8. String 1 small bead, 1 large bead, and 1 small bead on the 2 center cords.

Step 9. With the 3rd, 4th, 5th and 6th cords from either side, tie 2 Square Knots. With the 4 center cords, tie 2 Square Knots.

Step 10. String 1 small bead, 1 large bead and 1 small bead on the 4 center cords. With the 4 center cords, tie 1 Square Knot.

Step 11. With the 3 left cords, tie 1 Multiple-Strand Overhand Knot. With the next 3 left cords, tie 1 Multiple-Strand Overhand Knot. With the next 4 left cords, tie 1 Multiple-Strand Overhand Knot. Repeat this step on the right.

Step 12. With the 3 center cords, tie 1 Multiple-Strand Overhand Knot. String 2 small beads on each cord. Tie 1 Simple Overhand Knot, 2″ below the last row of knots. Trim all ends close to last knot.

Fig. 112

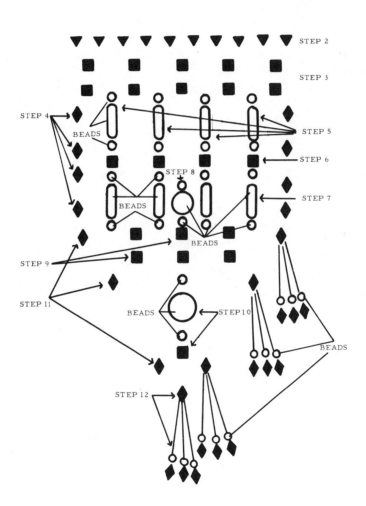

LACY JUTE NECKLACE

(See Figs. 113, 114 and Plate 19)

MATERIALS

54′ natural jute; 24 small beads.

METHOD

Step 1. Cut 6 knotting-cords, each 9′ long. Tie all the cords together in the center with 1 Multiple-Strand Overhand Knot. This will be the center-back of the necklace. Pin the knot to the knotting board so that half of the cords are on the far side of the knot, and half of the cords are on the near side of the knot.

Step 2. With the 4 center cords, tie 1 Square Knot.

Step 3. With the 4 left cords, tie 1 Alternating Square Knot.

Step 4. With the 4 right cords, tie 1 Alternating Square Knot.

Step 5. Repeat Steps 2, 3 and 4 six times. This will form 1 side of the necklace.

Step 6. Turn the cords around so that the knotted portion is on the far side of the Multiple-Strand Overhand Knot, and the unknotted cords are on the near side of the knot.

Step 7. Repeat Steps 2 through 5 to form the second side of the necklace.

Step 8. Lay the knotted portions side-by-side with the Multiple-Strand Overhand Knot in the rear and the unknotted cords at the front. With the 8 center cords, tie 2 Alternating Square Knots. These knots will join the necklace together in the front. Check to see that the opening formed is large enough to go over the head. If not, untie the 2 Alternating Square Knots and tie additional Alternating Square Knots on each side of the necklace.

Step 9. Tie 2 rows of Alternating Square Knots.

Step 10. With the 4 center cords, tie 1 Alternating Square Knot.

Steps 11 through 15 will form a diamond pattern of Diagonal Double Half Hitches.

Step 11. The 2 center cords become the *left* and *right core-cords*. The other 5 cords on the left become the *left knotting-cords*. The other 5 cords on the right become the *right knotting-cords*.

Step 12. Carry the right core-cord diagonally across the right knotting-cords. Tie the right knotting-cords around the right core-cord with Diagonal Double Half Hitches.

Step 13. Carry the left core-cord diagonally across the left knotting-cords. Tie the left knotting-cords around the left core-cord with Diagonal Double Half Hitches.

Step 14. Carry the right core-cord diagonally back to the center across the right knotting-cords. Tie the right knotting-cords around the right core-cord with Diagonal Double Half Hitches.

Step 15. Carry the left core-cord diagonally back to the center across the left knotting-cords. Tie the left knotting-cords around the left core-cord with Diagonal Double Half Hitches.

Step 16. With the 4 center cords, tie 1 Square Knot.

Step 17. String 2 beads on each cord. Tie 1 Simple Overhand Knot 2" below the last row of knots. Trim all ends to 1".

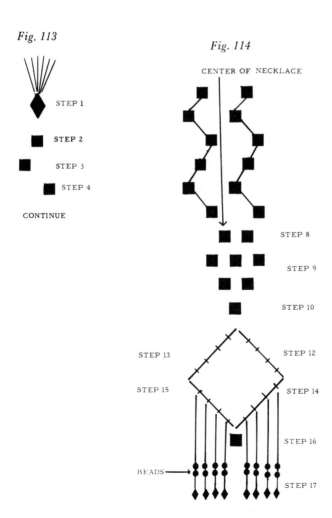

Fig. 113

Fig. 114

WOOL NECKLACE

(See Fig. 115 and Plate 33)

MATERIALS

48′ blue rug yarn; 8 red barrel beads.

METHOD

Step 1. Cut 8 cords, each 6′ long. Tie all cords together in the center with a Multiple-Strand Overhand Knot. This will be the center-back of the necklace. Pin the knot to the knotting board so that half of the cords are on the near side of the knot, and half of the cords are on the far side of the knot.

Step 2. With the 4 center cords, tie 2 Square Knots.

Step 3. Tie 2 Alternating Square Knots.

Step 4. Repeat Steps 2 and 3 until a total of 36 Square Knots have been tied. This will form one side of the necklace.

Step 5. Turn the cords around so that the knotted portion is on the far side of the Multiple-Strand Overhand Knot, and the unknotted cords are on the near side of that knot.

Step 6. Repeat Steps 2 through 4. This will form the second side of the necklace.

Step 7. Lay the knotted portions side-by-side with the Multiple-Strand Overhand Knot in the rear and the unknotted cords at the front. Leaving the outside cords on each side free, tie 1 row of Alternating Square Knots. These knots will join the necklace together in the front. Check to see that the opening formed is large enough to go over the head. If not, untie the row of Alternating Square Knots and tie additional Alternating Square Knots on each side of the necklace.

Step 8. With the 8 center cords, tie 2 Alternating Square Knots.

Step 9. With the 4 center cords, tie 1 Alternating Square Knot.

Steps 10 through 14 will form an "X" pattern of Diagonal Double Half Hitches.

Step 10. Divide the number of cords by half. The outside left cord becomes the *left core-cord*. The other 7 cords on the left become the *left knotting-cords*. The outside right cord becomes the *right core-cord*. The other 7 cords on the right become the *right knotting-cords*.

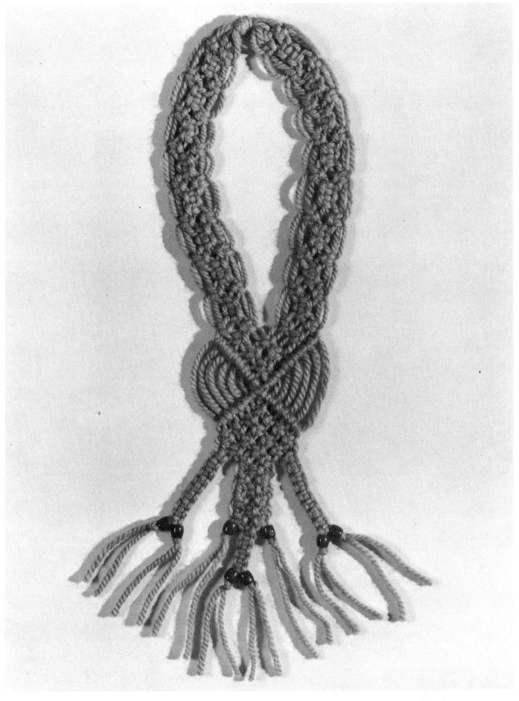

Plate 33. Wool Necklace. Soft, washable rug yarn was used to knot this delicately-patterned necklace, suitable for a man or a woman.

108

Fig. 115

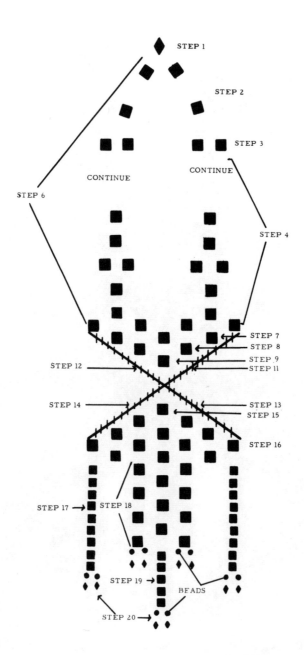

Step 11. Carry the right core-cord diagonally across the right knotting-cords. Tie the right knotting-cords around the right core-cord with Diagonal Double Half Hitches.

Step 12. Carry the left core-cord diagonally across the left knotting-cords. Tie the left knotting-cords around the left core-cord with Diagonal Double Half Hitches.

Step 13. Cross the left core-cord over the right core-cord and carry it diagonally over the right knotting-cords. Tie the right knotting-cords around the left core-cord with Diagonal Double Half Hitches.

Step 14. Take the right core-cord, which lies under the left core-cord, and carry it diagonally *over* the left knotting-cords. Tie the left knotting-cords around the right core-cord with Diagonal Double Half Hitches.

Step 15. With the 4 center cords, tie 1 Square Knot.

Step 16. Tie 4 rows of Alternating Square Knots.

Step 17. With the 4 left cords, tie 8 Square Knots. Repeat this step on the right.

Step 18. With the 8 center cords, tie 6 rows of Alternating Square Knots.

Step 19. With the 4 center cords, tie 5 Square Knots.

Step 20. Divide the cords into pairs. String 1 bead on each pair of cords. Tie 1 Double Strand Overhand Knot below each bead. Trim all ends to 4″.

INDIAN JUTE NECKLACE

(See Figs. 116, 117 and Plate 34)

MATERIALS

120′ natural jute; 8 large beads.

METHOD

Step 1. Cut 8 cords, each 15′ long. Lay the centers of the cords side-by-side on the knotting board. Begin knotting in the center of the cords.
Steps 2 through 6 will form an "X" pattern of Diagonal Double Half Hitches.

Step 2. Divide the number of cords in half. The outside left cord becomes the *left core-cord*. The other 3 cords on the left become the *left knotting-cords*. The outside right cord becomes the *right core-cord*. The other 3 cords on the right become the *right knotting-cords*.

Step 3. Carry the right core-cord diagonally across the right knotting-cords. Tie the right knotting-cords around the right core-cord with Diagonal Double Half Hitches.

Step 4. Carry the left core-cord diagonally across the left knotting-cords. Tie the left knotting-cords around the left core-cord with Diagonal Double Half Hitches.

Step 5. Cross the left core-cord over the right core-cord and carry it diagonally over the right knotting-cords. Tie the right knotting-cords around the left core-cord with Diagonal Double Half Hitches.

Step 6. Take the right core-cord, which lies under the left core-cord, and carry it diagonally *over* the left knotting-cords. Tie the left knotting-cords around the right core-cord with Diagonal Double Half Hitches. This "X" will be the center-back of the necklace.

Step 7. With the 4 center cords, tie 1 Square Knot. Tie 6 rows of Alternating Square Knots.

Step 8. Repeat Steps 2 through 7 three times. This will complete one side of the necklace.

Step 9. Remove the knotted portion from the knotting board. Place the center "X" at the top of the knotting board with the knotted portion away from you and the unknotted cords near you. Repeat Step 7. Repeat Steps 2 through 7 three times. This will complete the second side of the necklace.

Fig. 116

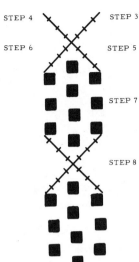

Step 10. Lay the 2 knotted portions side-by-side with all unknotted cords facing you. With the 4 center cords, tie 1 Square Knot. This knot will join the necklace together in the front. Check to see that the opening formed is large enough to go over the head. If not, untie this Square Knot and tie additional Alternating Square Knots on each side.

Fig. 117

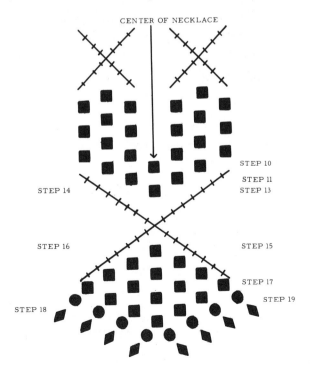

Step 11. With the 8 center cords, tie 2 Alternating Square Knots. With the 4 center cords, tie 1 Alternating Square Knot.

Steps 12 through 16 will form an "X" pattern of Diagonal Double Half Hitches.

Step 12. Divide the number of cords in half. The outside left cord becomes the *left core-cord*. The other 7 cords on the left become the *left knotting-cords*. The outside right cord becomes the *right core-cord*. The other 7 cords on the right become the *right knotting-cords*.

Step 13. Carry the right core-cord diagonally across the right knotting-cords. Tie the right knotting-cords around the right core-cord with Diagonal Double Half Hitches.

Step 14. Carry the left core-cord diagonally across the left knotting-cords. Tie the left knotting-cords around the left core-cord with Diagonal Double Half Hitches.

Step 15. Cross the left core-cord over the right core-cord and carry it diagonally over the right knotting-cords. Tie the right knotting-cords around the left core-cord with Diagonal Double Half Hitches.

Step 16. Take the right core-cord, which lies under the left core-cord, and carry it diagonally *over* the left knotting-cords. Tie the left knotting-cords around the right core-cord with Diagonal Double Half Hitches.

Step 17. With the 4 center cords, tie 1 Square Knot. Tie 3 rows of Alternating Square Knots, *increasing* each row by 1 Alternating Square Knot.

Step 18. Tie 3 rows of Alternating Square Knots, *decreasing* each row by 1 Alternating Square Knot.

Step 19. Divide the cords into pairs. String 1 bead on each pair of cords. Tie 1 Double-Strand Overhand Knot directly below each bead. Trim all ends close to the knot.

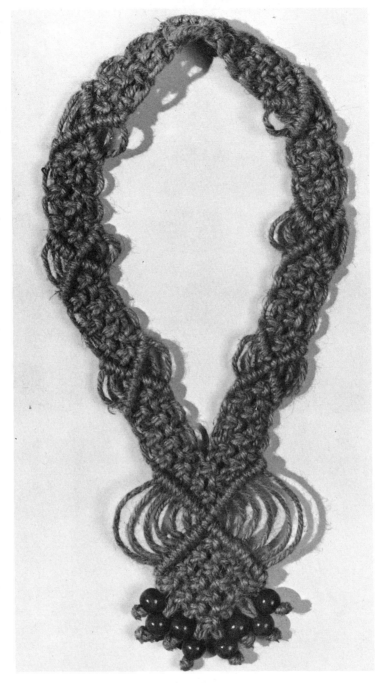

Plate 34. Indian Jute Necklace. This handsome man's neckpiece was knotted from heavy natural jute and is trimmed with large wooden beads. Make it for a woman in a lighter, more refined cord, such as rattail. Courtesy William Baker.

Plate 35. Suspenders. A giant "X" pattern worked in a lightweight rayon cord makes this unusual fashion accessory. Courtesy Walco.

SUSPENDERS

(See Fig. 118 and Plate 35)

MATERIALS

144' green rayon cord; 96' white rayon cord; 96' blue rayon cord; 4 suspender clasps.

METHOD

Step 1. Cut 3 green, 2 white and 2 blue knotting-cords, each 24' long. Fold all the knotting-cords in half and mount them on the shank of one suspender clasp in the following sequence: 1 green, 1 white, 1 blue, 1 green, 1 blue, 1 white, 1 green.

Step 2. The 2 center cords become the *left* and *right core-cords*. The other 6 cords on the left become the *left knotting-cords*. The other 6 cords on the right become the *right knotting-cords*.

Step 3. Carry the right core-cord diagonally across the right knotting-cords. Tie the right knotting-cords around the right core-cord with Diagonal Double Half Hitches.

Step 4. Carry the left core-cord diagonally across the left knotting-cords. Tie the left knotting-cords around the left core-cord with Diagonal Double Half Hitches.

Step 5. Repeat Steps 2, 3 and 4 two times.

Step 6. Divide the number of cords in half. The outside left cord becomes the *left core-cord*. The outside right cord becomes the right core-cord. The other 6 cords on the left become the *left knotting-cords*. The other 6 cords on the right become the *right knotting-cords*.

Step 7. Carry the right core-cord diagonally across the right knotting-cords. Tie the right knotting-cords around the right core-cord with Diagonal Double Half Hitches.

Step 8. Carry the left core-cord diagonally across the left knotting-cords. Tie the left knotting-cords around the left core-cord with Diagonal Double Half Hitches.

Step 9. Repeat Steps 6, 7 and 8 two times.

Step 10. Cross the left core-cord over the right core-cord and carry it diagonally over the right knotting-cords. Tie the right knotting-cords around the left core-cord with Diagonal Double Half Hitches.

116

Step 11. Take the right core-cord, which lies under the left core-cord, and carry it diagonally *over* the left knotting-cords. Tie the left knotting-cords around the right core-cord with Diagonal Double Half Hitches.

Step 12. Repeat Steps 10 and 11 two times.

Step 13. Repeat Steps 3 through 11 eight times.

Step 14. With the 4 left cords, tie 7 Square Knots. Repeat this step on the right.

Step 15. The 4 center cords become *core-cords*. Tie 7 Square Knots over these 4 core-cords. Carry the cords around the shank of a second suspender clasp and thread them through the back of several knots. Trim all the ends close to the back of the piece and glue in place.

Step 16. Repeat Steps 1 through 15 for the other side of the suspenders. Tie the 2 sides together at a convenient spot in the back with a short piece of cord, using 1 Simple Overhand Knot.

Fig. 118

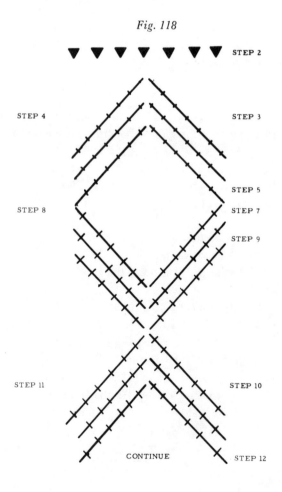

SEASHELL BRACELET

(See Fig. 119 and Plate 36)

MATERIALS

8′ white cable cord; 8′ red cable cord; 18′ yellow cable cord; 7 small seashells.

METHOD

Step 1. Cut 1 yellow holding-cord 6′ long. Cut 2 white, 2 red and 3 yellow knotting-cords, each 4′ long. String 1 shell on the holding-cord and position it in the center of the cord. Fold all the knotting-cords in half and mount them on the holding-cord with Clove Hitches in the following sequence: 1 yellow, 1 red, 1 white, 1 yellow (this Clove Hitch will go *around* the shell) 1 white, 1 red, 1 yellow. Pull the shell above the line of Clove Hitches so that it may be used to button the ends of the bracelet together.

Step 2. Following the directions for the Cable Cord Bracelet, with the following exceptions:

A. Fold the ends of the holding-cord down beside the knotting-cords and the ends become the *right outside* and *left outside core-cords.*

B. Omit Step 2.

C. Tie 7 complete diamond patterns down the center of the bracelet.

D. Repeat Steps 9, 10 and 11 *three times.*

E. Add 1 seashell to the 2 core-cords in Step 12. Additional seashells may be added at random to the face of the bracelet.

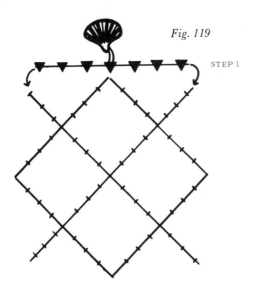

Fig. 119

STEP 1

Plate 36. Seashell Bracelet. Seashells enliven this simple cable cord bracelet. Beads, charms or other trinkets would be equally effective. Courtesy Abbey Sperber.

Plate 37. Cable Cord Bracelet. Natural cable cord presents a bold diamond pattern of Diagonal Double Half Hitches. Courtesy Abbey Sperber.

CABLE CORD BRACELET

(Fig. 120 and Plate 37)

MATERIALS

33′ cable cord; 1 small bead.

METHOD

Step 1. Cut 1 holding-cord 12″ long. Cut 8 knotting-cords, each 4′ long. String 1 bead on the holding-cord and position it in the center of the cord. Fold all the knotting-cords in half and mount them on the holding-cord with Clove Hitches, 4 on each side of the bead. Pull the bead above the line of Clove Hitches so that it may be used to button the bracelet.

Step 2. Cut 1 core-cord 12″ long. Lay it across all the knotting-cords directly below the Clove Hitches. Tie all the knotting-cords around the core-cord with Horizontal Double Half Hitches.

Step 3. The 2 center cords become the *right center* and *left center core-cords*. The 2 outside cords become the *right outside* and *left outside core-cords*.

Step 4. Carry the right center core-cord diagonally across the 3 knotting-cords directly to its right. Tie these 3 knotting-cords around the right center core-cord with Diagonal Double Half Hitches.

Step 5. Carry the left center core-cord diagonally across the 3 knotting-cords directly to its left. Tie these 3 knotting-cords around the left center core-cord with Diagonal Double Half Hitches.

Step 6. Carry the right outside core-cord diagonally across the 3 knotting-cords directly to its left. Tie these 3 knotting-cords around the right outside core-cord with Diagonal Double Half Hitches.

Step 7. Carry the left outside core-cord diagonally across the 3 knotting-cords directly to its right. Tie these 3 knotting-cords around the left outside core-cord with Diagonal Double Half Hitches.

Step 8. Cross the core-cords over one another and continue tying Diagonal Double Half Hitches until there are 5 complete diamond patterns down the center of the bracelet.

Step 9. Divide the number of cords in half. The outside left cord becomes the *left core-cord*. The other 7 cords on the left become the left knotting-cords. The outside right cord becomes the *right core-cord*. The other 7 cords on the right become the right knotting-cords.

Step 10. Carry the right core-cord diagonally across the right knotting-cords. Tie the right knotting-cords around the right core-cord with Diagonal Double Half Hitches.

Step 11. Carry the left core-cord diagonally across the left knotting-cords. Tie the left knotting-cords around the left core-cord with Diagonal Double Half Hitches.

Step 12. Tie the 2 core-cords together in the center with 1 Double-Strand Overhand Knot, leaving enough space for the bead to be buttoned through the loop. Carry the balance of the cords to the reverse side and thread them through the back of several knots. Trim all the ends close to the back of the piece and glue in place.

Fig. 120

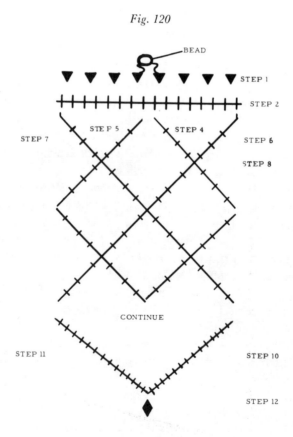

Plate 38. Rayon Bracelet. Triple rows of Diagonal Double Half Hitches form large "X" patterns. Courtesy Abbey Sperber.

RAYON BRACELET

(See Fig. 121 and Plate 38)

MATERIALS

32′ orange rayon cord; 32′ brown rayon cord; 1 large button.

METHOD

Step 1. Cut 1 brown holding-cord 8′ long. Cut 4 orange and 3 brown knotting-cords, each 8′ long. Fold all the knotting-cords in half and mount them on the center of the holding-cord with Clove Hitches in the following sequence: 2 orange, 3 brown, 2 orange. Angle the center of the holding-cord down in the middle to form a slight "V" shape. Fold the ends of the holding-cord down beside the knotting-cords.

Step 2. Divide the number of cords in half. The outside left cord becomes the *left core-cord*. The other 7 cords on the left become the *left knotting-cords*. The outside right cord becomes the *right core-cord*. The other 7 cords on the right become the *right knotting-cords*.

Step 3. Carry the right core-cord diagonally across the right knotting-cords. Tie the right knotting-cords around the right core-cord with Diagonal Double Half Hitches.

Step 4. Carry the left core-cord diagonally across the left knotting-cords. Tie the left knotting-cords around the left core-cord with Diagonal Double Half Hitches.

Step 5. Repeat Steps 2, 3 and 4 one time.

Step 6. The 2 center cords become the *left* and *right core-cords*. The other 7 cords on the left become the *left knotting-cords*. The other 7 cords on the right become the *right knotting-cords*.

Step 7. Carry the right core-cord diagonally across the right knotting-cords. Tie the right knotting-cords around the right core-cord with Diagonal Double Half Hitches.

Step 8. Carry the left core-cord diagonally across the left knotting-cords. Tie the left knotting-cords around the left core-cord with Diagonal Double Half Hitches.

Step 9. Repeat Steps 6, 7 and 8, two times.

Step 10. Repeat Steps 2, 3 and 4, three times.

Step 11. Repeat Steps 6, 7 and 8, three times.

Step 12. Repeat Steps 2, 3 and 4, eight times.

Step 13. Carry all the cords to the reverse side and thread them through the back of several knots. Trim all the ends close to the back of the piece and glue in place. Attach a small loop of brown rayon to the top of the bracelet. Attach a button to the pointed end of the bracelet.

Fig. 121

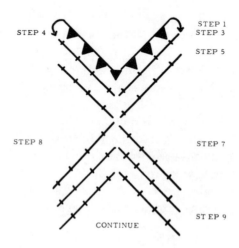

Fig. 122

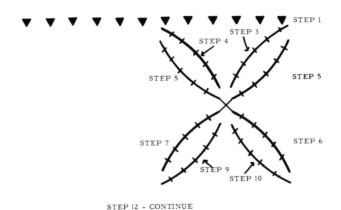

STEP 1
STEP 3
STEP 4
STEP 5
STEP 5
STEP 7
STEP 6
STEP 9
STEP 10

STEP 12 - CONTINUE

LEAF PATTERN EYEGLASS CASE

(See Fig. 122 and Plate 39)

MATERIALS

19' rust Lily Jute-Tone; 18' gold Lily Jute-Tone; felt lining material.

METHOD

Step 1. Cut 1 rust holding-cord 6″ long. Cut 6 rust and 6 gold knotting-cords, each 3' long. Fold all the knotting-cords in half and mount them in the center of the holding-cord with Clove Hitches in the following sequence: 3 rust, 6 gold, 3 rust.
Divide the number of cords in half. Steps 2 through 10 will be worked on the 12 left cords.

Step 2. Divide the 12 left cords in half. The outside left-cord becomes the *left core-cord*. The other 5 cords on the left become the *left knotting-cords*. The outside right cord becomes the *right core-cord*. The other 5 cords on the right become the *right knotting-cords*.

Step 3. Carry the right core-cord diagonally across the right knotting-cords. Curve the core-cord *upward* slightly, in the center. Tie the right knotting-cords around the right core-cord with Diagonal Double Half Hitches.

Step 4. Carry the left core-cord diagonally across the left knotting-cords. Curve the core-cord *upward* slightly in the center. Tie the right knotting-cords around the right core-cord with Diagonal Double Half Hitches.

Step 5. Repeat Steps 2, 3 and 4, curving the core cord *downward* slightly in the center, instead of upward.

Step 6. Cross the left core-cord over the right core-cord and carry it diagonally over the right knotting-cords. Curve the core-cord *upward* slightly in the center. Tie the right knotting-cords around the left core-cord with Diagonal Double Half Hitches.

Step 7. Take the right core-cord, which lies under the left core-cord, and carry it diagonally *over* the left knotting-cords. Curve the core-cord *upward* slightly in the center. Tie the left knotting-cords around the right core-cord with Diagonal Double Half Hitches.

Step 8. The 2 center cords become the *right* and *left core-cords*. The other 5 cords on the left become the *left knotting-cords*. The other 5 cords on the right become the *right knotting-cords.*

Step 9. Cross the left core-cord over the right core-cord and carry it diagonally over the right knotting-cords. Curve the core-cord *downward* slightly in the center. Tie the right knotting-cords around the left core-cord with Diagonal Double Half Hitches.

Step 10. Take the right core-cord, which lies under the left core-cord, and carry it diagonally *over* the left knotting-cords. Curve the core-cord *downward* slightly in the center. Tie the left knotting-cords around the right core-cord with Diagonal Double Half Hitches.

Step 11. Repeat Steps 2 through 10, with the 12 cords on the right.

Step 12. Cross the 2 center cords over one another. Repeat Steps 2 through 11, three times.

Step 13. Cut 1 rust core-cord 6″ long. Lay it horizontally across all the cords. Tie all the cords around the core-cord with Horizontal Double Half Hitches. Carry all the cords to the reverse side and thread them through the back of several knots. Trim all the ends close to the back of the piece and glue in place.

Step 14. Repeat Steps 1 through 13 for the reverse side of the eyeglass case. If a lining is desired, cut 2 pieces of felt the same size as the finished pieces. Lay 1 knotted piece, face down, on the table. Lay the 2 pieces of felt on top. Lay the second knotted piece on top of the felt, face up. Carefully stitch around the sides and bottom. Place the stitches between the knots so that the thread does not show.

Plate 39. Striped Eyeglass Case (top). Leaf-Pattern Eyeglass Case (lower left). Jute Eyeglass Case (lower right). Quick and economical projects, they make excellent personal gifts. Striped Eyeglass Case and Leaf-Pattern Eyeglass Case Courtesy Terry Schwartz.

STRIPED EYEGLASS CASE

(See Fig. 123 and Plate 39)

MATERIALS

21' red rayon cord; 12' white rayon cord; 12' blue rayon cord; felt lining material.

METHOD

Step 1. Cut 1 red holding-cord 6" long. Cut 12 red core-cords, each 6" long. Cut 6 red, 4 white and 4 blue knotting-cords, each, 18" long. Fold all the knotting-cords in half and mount them on the holding-cord with Clove Hitches in the following sequence: 2 red, 2 white, 2 blue, 2 red, 2 blue, 2 white, 2 red.

Step 2. Tie 3 rows of Interlocking Square Knots.

Step 3. Lay 1 red core-cord across all the knotting-cords. Tie the knotting-cords around the core-cord with Horizontal Double Half Hitches. Repeat this step, one more time.

Step 4. Repeat Steps 2 and 3, five times.

Step 5. Carry all the cords to the reverse side and thread them through the back of several knots. Trim all the ends close to the back of the piece and glue in place.

Step 6. Repeat Steps 1 through 5, for the other half of the eyeglass case. If a lining is desired, cut 2 pieces of felt the same size as the finished pieces. Lay 1 knotted piece, face down, on the table. Lay the 2 pieces of felt on top. Lay the second knotted piece on top of the felt, face up. Carefully stitch around the sides and bottom. Place the stitches between the knots so that the thread does not show.

Fig. 123

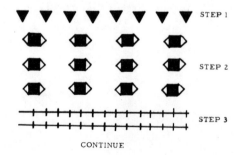

CONTINUE

Fig. 124

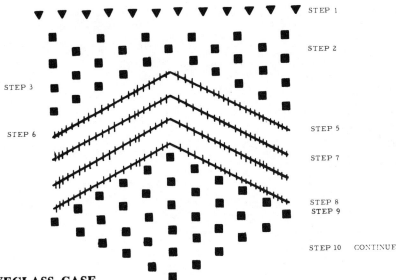

JUTE EYEGLASS CASE

(See Fig. 124 and Plate 39)

MATERIALS

25' white Lily Jute-Tone; 12' rose Lily Jute-Tone; felt lining material.

METHOD

Step 1. Cut 1 white holding-cord 6" long. Cut 8 white and 4 rose knot-ting-cords, each 5' long. Fold all the knotting-cords in half and mount them on the holding-cord with Clove Hitches in the following sequence: 4 white, 4 rose, 4 white.

Step 2. Beginning with the outside 4 cords on either side, tie 1 row of Square Knots. Tie 2 rows of Alternating Square Knots.

Step 3. Leaving the 2 left cords free, tie 2 Alternating Square Knots. With the 8 left cords, tie 2 Alternating Square Knots. Leaving the 2 left cords free, tie 1 Alternating Square Knot. With the 4 left cords, tie 1 Alternating Square Knot. Repeat this step on the right.

Step 4. The 2 center cords become the *left* and *right core-cords*. The other 11 cords on the left become the *left knotting-cords*. The other 11 cords on the right become the *right knotting-cords*.

Step 5. Carry the right core-cord diagonally across the right knotting-cords. Tie the right knotting-cords around the right core-cord with Diagonal Double Half Hitches.

Step 6. Carry the left core-cord diagonally across the left knotting-cords. Tie the left knotting-cords around the left core-cord with Diagonal Double Half Hitches.

Step 7. Repeat Steps 4 through 6, three times.

Step 8. With the 4 center cords, tie 1 Square Knot. Tie 4 rows of Alternating Square Knots.

Step 9. Tie 1 more row of Alternating Square Knots. This becomes the center of the design.

Step 10. Repeat Steps 2 through 8, in *reverse* order.

Step 11. Carry all the cords to the reverse side and thread them through the back of several knots.

Step 12. Repeat Steps 1 through 13, for the other half of the eyeglass case. If a lining is desired, cut 2 pieces of felt the same size as the finished pieces. Lay 1 knotted piece, face down, on the table. Lay the 2 pieces of felt on top. Lay the second knotted piece on top of the felt, face up. Carefully stitch around the sides and bottom. Place the stitches between the knots so that the thread does not show.

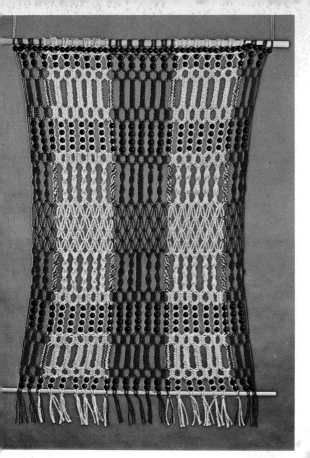

Plate VII. Room Divider. A basic red and white color scheme accented by shiny blue beads, with two simple knots, the Square Knot and the Half Knot.

Plate VIII. Hand-dyed Sisal Wall Hanging. By manipulation of the cords and by use of the Diagonal Double Half Hitch the colors make an interesting pattern. Courtesy Irene Michaud.

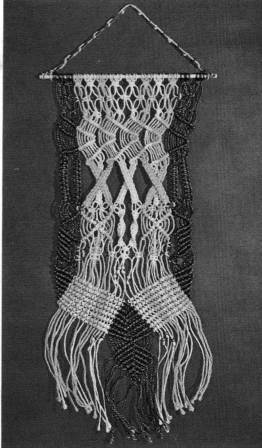

Plate XI. Hanging Lamp. Delicate and heavily knotted patterns are contrasted. Notice how the gold and rust cords change places at intervals.

Plate X. Sisal and Shell Wall Hanging for a patio or terrace. Each knotted section was dyed after the knotting was completed.

(left)
Plate IX. Radiating Bands Sash, Chevron Sash, Triple "V" Sash, "V" Sash, Banded Sash and Diamond Sash. Simple upholsterer's cable cord has been hand-dyed in unusual tones and shadings.

Plate XIII. (Top to bottom) Cable Cord Belt. Beaded Jute Belt. Wide Jute Belt. Banded Belt. Beaded Jute Sash. Readily available materials, such as jute and cable cord, were dyed to produce lovely color combinations. Belts and Sashes courtesy William Baker.

Plate XII. Party Tunic. Shiny rayon cord and sparkling beads combine in this unusual party tunic. The very long fringe and beads are lovely in motion. Great for the dance scene!

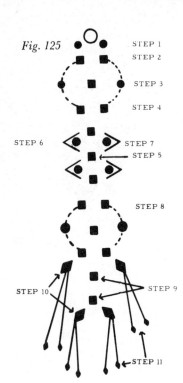

Fig. 125

STEP 1
STEP 2
STEP 3
STEP 4
STEP 6   STEP 7
STEP 5
STEP 8
STEP 10   STEP 9
STEP 11

RATTAIL KEY RING

(See Fig. 125 and Plate 40)

MATERIALS

Key Ring; 6′ gold rattail;
6′ purple rattail; 20 beads.

METHOD

Step 1. Cut 2 gold and 2 purple cords, each 3′ long. Thread the 4 cords through the small ring of the key ring. Center the ring on the cords. Spread the cords so that the gold cords are on the outside, and the purple cords are on the inside. String 1 bead on each of the outside cords.

Step 2. With the 4 left cords, tie 1 Square Knot. Repeat this step on the right.

Step 3. With the 4 center cords, tie 1 Alternating Square Knot. String 1 bead on each side of the outside cords.

Step 4. Repeat Step 2.

Step 5. With the 4 center cords, tie 3 Square Knots.

Step 6. String 1 bead on the left cord. With the 2 left cords, tie 1 Reversed Double Half Hitch, placing the bead in the center of the knot. Repeat this step, one more time.

Step 7. Repeat Step 6 on the right.

Step 8. Repeat the above steps in the following sequence: 2, 3, 2.

Step 9. With the 4 center cords, tie 2 Square Knots.

Step 10. Divide the cords into pairs. Tie 1 Double-Strand Overhand Knot on each pair of cords.

Step 11. String 1 bead on each cord and tie 1 Simple Overhand Knot 2″ below the last knot. Trim cords close to last knot.

Plate 40. Cable Cord Key Ring (top). Rattail Key Ring (center). Jute Key Ring (bottom). These small key rings are excellent bazaar or gift items. Each requires a minimum of cord (great for using up those odds and ends).

CABLE CORD KEY RING

(See Fig. 126 and Plate 40)

MATERIALS

Key Ring; 12′ cable cord; 28 small wooden beads.

METHOD

Step 1. Cut 2 cords, each 3′ long. Thread the cords through the small ring of the key ring. Spread cords so that they lay side-by-side. The 2 center ends should measure 8″ and the 2 outside ends should measure 28″. The 2 short ends will be core-cords and the 2 long ends will be the knotting-cords.

Step 2. Tie 2 Reversed Double Half Hitches over the 2 core-cords. String 1 bead on the left knotting-cord and tie 1 Reversed Double Half Hitch over the 2 core-cords. Repeat this step on the right.

Step 3. Repeat Step 2, sixteen more times.

Step 4. Tie the left core-cord and the left knotting-cord together with 1 Double-Strand Overhand Knot. Repeat this step on the right.

Step 5. Cut 1 cord 3′ long. Thread the cord through the small ring of the key ring, to the left of the sinnet tied in Steps 1 through 4. Spread the cord so that the ends lay side-by-side. The outside end should measure 28″. The inside end should measure 8″. The short end will be the core-cord and the long end with be the knotting-cord.

Step 6. Tie 6 Half Hitches. String 1 bead on the core-cord. Repeat this step four more times.

Step 7. Tie the core-cord and knotting-cords together with 1 Double-Strand Overhand Knot directly below the last bead.

Step 8. Repeat Steps 5 through 7 on the right side of the original sinnet. Trim all ends to 1½″.

Fig. 126

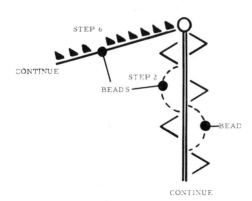

Fig. 127

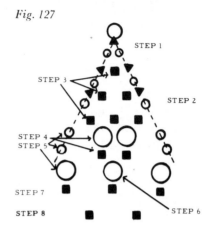

STEP 1

STEP 3

STEP 2

STEP 4
STEP 5

STEP 7

STEP 6

STEP 8

JUTE KEY RING

(See Fig. 127 and Plate 40)

MATERIALS

Key Ring; 15′ Lily Jute-Tone; 12 small beads; 5 medium beads.

METHOD

Step 1. Cut 6 cords, each 30″ long. Fold 1 cord in half and mount it on the small ring of the key ring with a Clove Hitch. Thread a 2nd cord through the small ring of the key ring. Center the ring on this cord. Lay this cord horizontally on the knotting board. This cord will be the holding-cord for the balance of the cords. String 2 small beads on the holding-cord, 1 on each side of the key ring.

Step 2. Fold 2 cords in half and mount them on the holding cord with Clove Hitches, 1 on the outside of each bead. String 2 small beads on the holding-cord, 1 on the outside of each cord. Repeat this step, one more time.

Step 3. Fold the ends of the holding cord down so that it forms an inverted "V". With the 4 center cords, tie 1 Square Knot. With the 8 center cords, tie 2 Alternating Square Knots. Tie 1 row of 3 Alternating Square Knots.

Step 4. String 1 medium bead on the 4th and 5th cords from the left. Using these 2 cords as core-cords, tie 1 Square Knot below the bead. Repeat this step on the right.

Step 5. String 2 small beads on the left cord. String 1 medium bead on the 2nd and 3rd cords from the left. Repeat this step on the right.

Step 6. String 1 large bead on the 2 center cords.

Step 7. Using the 2 cords that have been strung through the large beads as core-cords, tie 1 Square Knot below each of the large beads.

Step 8. With the 8 center cords, tie 2 Alternating Square Knots. Trim all ends to 1½″.

CABLE CORD BAG

(7" by 8". See Fig. 128 and Plate 41)

MATERIALS

151' cable cord.

METHOD

Step 1. Cut 1 holding-cord 12" long. Cut 24 knotting-cords, each 6' long. Fold all the knotting-cords in half and mount them on the holding-cord with Clove Hitches.

Step 2. Divide the cords into groups of 4. Tie 4 Square Knots on each group of 4 cords.

Step 3. Tie 20 rows of Alternating Square Knots.

Step 4. Repeat Steps 2 and 3.

Step 5. Carry all the cords to the reverse side and thread them through the back of several knots. Trim all ends close to the back of the piece and glue in place. Fold the bag in half. Sew the 2 sides together. Place stitches between the knots so that the thread does not show.

Fig. 128

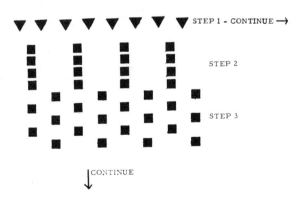

Step 6. Cut 2 knotting-cords, each 3′ long. Tie a sinnet of Single Chain Knots. Sew the ends of this sinnet to the inside top edge of the bag on the side folds.

Plate 41. Cable Cord Bag. The strong, beautiful pattern of Alternating Square Knots is shown to advantage in this small, practical bag. Worked in natural cable cord, it is washable and very durable. Courtesy Abbey Sperber.

Plate 42. Wool Bag. A small shoulder bag was made with washable rug yarn. It requires a minimum amount of material.

WOOL BAG

(See Fig. 129, Plate 42 and Color Plate I)

MATERIALS

135′ red rug yarn; 168′ blue rug yarn; felt lining material.

METHOD

Step 1. Cut 1 red holding-cord 12″ long. Cut 12 blue and 6 red knotting-cords, each 14′ long. Fold all the knotting-cords in half and mount them on the holding-cord with Clove Hitches in the following sequence: 6 blue, 6 red, 6 blue.

Step 2. Beginning with the outside 4 cords on either side, tie 1 row of Square Knots. Tie 2 rows of Alternating Square Knots.

Step 3. The 2 center red cords become the *left* and *right core-cords*. The other 5 red cords on the left become the *left knotting-cords*. The other 5 red cords on the right become the *right knotting-cords*.

Step 4. Carry the right core-cord diagonally across the right knotting-cords. Tie the right knotting-cords around the right core-cord with Diagonal Double Half Hitches.

Step 5. Carry the left core-cord diagonally across the left knotting-cords. Tie the left knotting-cords around the left core-cord with Diagonal Double Half Hitches.

Step 6. Repeat Steps 3 through 5 with the blue cords on each side. Wrap the red and blue core-cords once around each other where they adjoin.

Step 7. Carry the right red core-cord diagonally back to the center across the right red knotting-cords. Tie the right knotting-cords around the right core-cord with Diagonal Double Half Hitches.

Step 8. Carry the left red core-cord diagonally back to the center across the left red knotting-cords. Tie the left knotting-cords around the left core-cord with Diagonal Double Half Hitches.

Step 9. Repeat Steps 7 and 8, with the blue cords, on each side.

Step 10. With the 4 center red cords, tie 1 Square Knot. With the 8 center red cords, tie 2 Alternating Square Knots. Repeat this step, with the blue cords, on each side.

Step 11. Tie 3 rows of Alternating Square Knots.

Step 12. With the 8 center red cords, tie 2 Alternating Square Knots. With the 4 center red cords, tie 1 Alternating Square Knot. Repeat this step, with the blue cords, on each side.

Step 13. Repeat Steps 3 through 11, three more times.

Step 14. Continue tying rows of Alternating Square Knots, decreasing each row by 1 Alternating Square Knot until a point is formed. Carry all the cords to the reverse side and thread them through the back of several knots. Trim all the ends close to the back of the piece and glue down.

Step 15. Lay the project face down on a table, with the point away from you. Cut lining felt the same size as the project. Baste the lining fabric to the edge of the knotted piece. Fold the end with the holding-cord away from you, toward the end with the point. Fold over at the bottom of the second row of diamond patterns that was formed with the Diagonal Double Half Hitches. Sew the sides of the pouch together. Fold the flap over the front of the bag. A snap may be added to the inside of the flap.

Step 16. To form a handle, cut 8 red cords, each 6 feet long. Tie all the cords together with 1 Multiple-Strand Overhand Knot 3″ from one end. Tie rows of Alternating Square Knots until the desired length is achieved. Tie 1 Multiple-Strand Overhand Knot below the last row of Alternating Square Knots. Trim all ends to 3″. To attach the handle, sew the Multiple-Strand Overhand Knots to the top edges of the bag.

Fig. 129

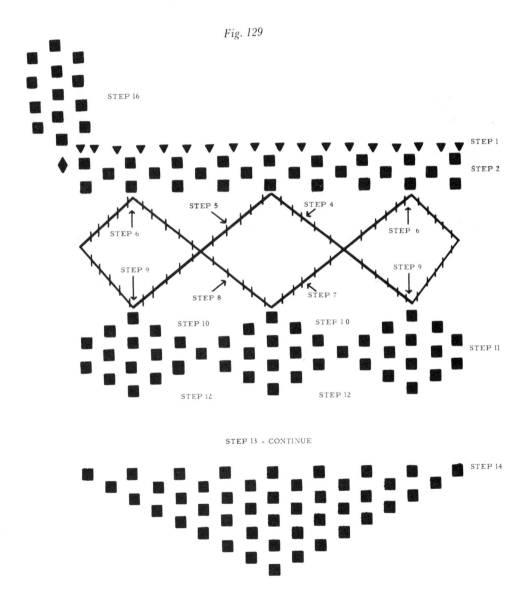

RAYON BAG

(See Fig. 130, Plate 43 and Color Plate I)

MATERIALS

64′ green rayon cord; 63′ white rayon cord; 63′ blue rayon cord.

METHOD

Step 1. Cut 1 green holding-cord 12″ long. Cut 8 green, 8 blue and 9 white knotting-cords, each 7′ long. Fold all the knotting-cords in half and mount them on the holding-cord with Clove Hitches in the following sequence: 1 green, 1 white, 3 blue, 3 white, 3 green, 1 blue, 1 white, 1 blue, 3 green, 3 white, 3 blue, 1 white, 1 green.

Step 2. Divide the cords into groups of 4. Tie 3 Square Knots on each group of 4 cords.

Step 3. Leaving the first 2 cords on either side free, divide the balance of the cords into groups of 4. Tie 6 Half Knots on each group of 4 cords.

Step 4. Divide the cords into groups of 4. Tie 6 Half Knots on each group of 4 cords.

Step 5. Leaving the first 2 cords on each side free, tie 1 row of Square Knots.

Step 6. Tie 8 rows of Alternating Square Knots.

Step 7. Repeat Step 2.

Step 8. Leaving the first 2 cords on each side free, divide the balance of the cords into groups of 4. Tie 3 Square Knots on each group of 4 cords.

Step 9. Beginning with the outside 4 cords on either side, tie 1 row of Alternating Square Knots.

Step 10. Tie 12 rows of Alternating Square Knots.

Step 11. Repeat the above steps in the following sequence: 8, 2, 5, 6, 4, 3, 2.

Step 12. Carry all the cords to the reverse side and thread them through the back of several knots. Trim all the ends close to the back of the piece and glue in place.

Step 13. Fold the knotted piece in half. Sew the 2 sides together. Place stitches between the knots so that the thread does not show.

Step 14. Cut 1 blue and 1 green knotting cord, each 7′ long. Tie a sinnet of Single Chain Knots. Sew the ends of this sinnet to the inside top edge of the bag on the side folds.

Fig. 130

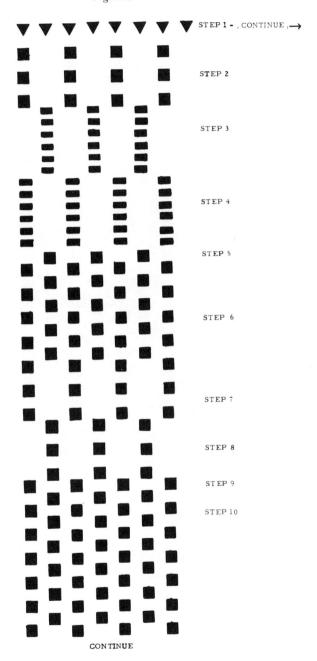

STEP 1 - , CONTINUE ⟶

STEP 2

STEP 3

STEP 4

STEP 5

STEP 6

STEP 7

STEP 8

STEP 9

STEP 10

CONTINUE

Plate 43. Rayon Bag. Multicolored rayon cords make an attractive striped shoulder bag. Because of the small cord and close knots, no lining is needed. Courtesy Walco.

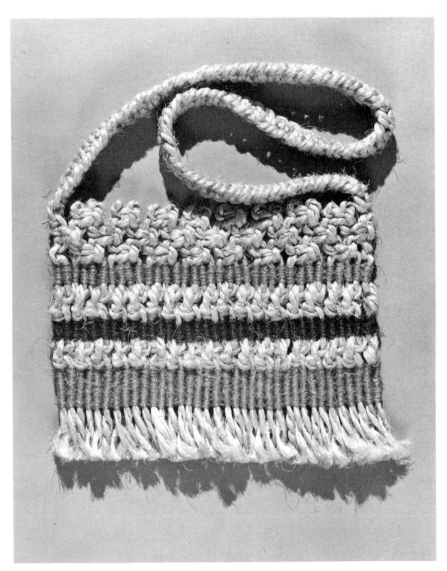

Plate 44. Sisal Tote Bag. Made with a heavy three-ply Africal Sisal and heavy jute, the bag will provide the owner with years of service.

142

SISAL TOTE BAG

(See Fig. 131, Plate 44 and Color Plate I)

MATERIALS

176′ of ⅛″ sisal; 495′ gold Lily Jute-Tone; 135′ rust Lily Jute-Tone

METHOD

Step 1. This step will form a sinnet of Alternating Half Hitches which will be used for the handle. Cut 2 sisal core-cords, each 75″ long. Cut 2 sisal knotting-cords, each 2′ long. Place one end of each of the 4 cords side-by-side, with the core-cords in the center. Begin knotting 21″ from these ends. Tie 34″ of Alternating Half Hitches over the 2 core-cords. This should leave 21″ unknotted at both ends of all 4 cords.

Step 2. Cut 32 sisal knotting-cords 50″ long. Fold the knotting-cords in half and pin the fold to the knotting board in the following sequence: 8 knotting-cords, 4 unknotted ends of the handle, 16 knotting cords, the other 4 ends of the handle, 8 knotting cords.

Step 3. Beginning with the outside 4 cords on either side, tie 1 row of Square Knots.

Step 4. Tie 2 rows of Alternating Square Knots.

Step 5. Cut 1 gold jute knotting cord 45′ long. Beginning at either side, tie 1 row of Vertical Double Half Hitches. Repeat this step, two more times.

Step 6. Divide the cords into pairs. Tie 2 Single Chain Knots on each pair of cords.

Step 7. Repeat Step 5, three times, using rust instead of gold jute.

Step 8. Repeat Step 6.

Step 9. Repeat Step 5, eight times.

Step 10. Trim all ends to 2″. Remove piece from knotting board. Fold so that the 2 sides meet in the back. With heavy thread sew the 2 sides together in the back. Sew the bottom closed on the last row of Vertical Double Half Hitches. Place stitches between the knots so that the thread does not show.

Fig. 131

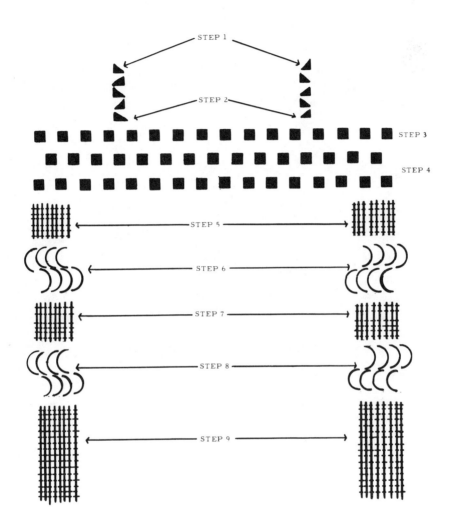

Plate 45. Tote Bag Appliqué. Frequently macrame can be added to manufactured articles to make them unique. In this case, a simple tote bag has a macrame appliqué of rug yarn sewn on front. It could be applied to vests, coats, pillows, etc.

TOTE BAG APPLIQUE

(See Fig. 132 and Plate 45)

MATERIALS

Tote Bag; 135½' red rug yarn; 60' blue rug yarn.

METHOD

Step 1. Cut 1 red holding-cord 18" long. Cut 24 red and 12 blue knotting-cords, each 5' long. Fold all the knotting-cords in half and mount them on the holding-cord with Clove Hitches in the following sequence: 12 red, 12 blue, 12 red.

Step 2. Leaving the 2 outside cords on each side free, tie 1 row of Square Knots. Tie 1 row of Alternating Square Knots.

Step 3. With the 4 center blue cords, tie 1 Square Knot. With the blue cords, tie 5 rows of Alternating Square Knots, *increasing* each row by 1 Alternating Square Knot. Tie 5 rows of Alternating Square Knots, *decreasing* each row by 1 Alternating Square Knot.

Step 4. Repeat Step 3 with the red cords.

Step 5. Tie 2 rows of Alternating Square Knots across *all* cords.

Step 6. Repeat Steps 3 and 4. Trim all ends to 1½". Appliqué the knotted piece to the face of the tote bag.

Step 7. Cut 2 red core-cords 2' long. Cut 2 red knotting-cords 5' long. Arrange the cords on the knotting board with the 2 core-cords in the center. Tie all the cords together with 1 Multiple-Strand Overhand Knot, 3" from one end of the cords. Tie 19 Square Knots. Tie all the cords together with 1 Multiple-Strand Overhand Knot. Tie 19 Square Knots. Tie all the cords together with 1 Multiple-Strand Overhand Knot. Trim the ends to 3". Appliqué this sinnet to the top of the knotted piece to cover the holding-cord.

Fig. 132

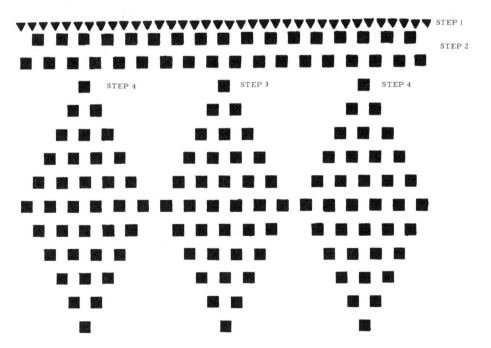

Fig. 132

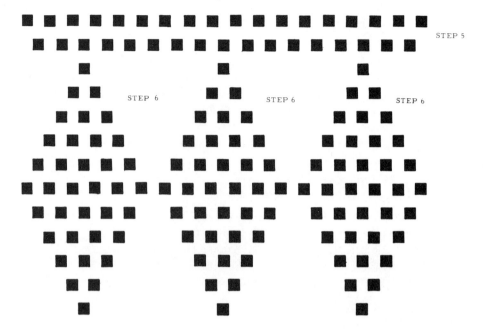

PARTY TUNIC

(Medium Size. See Fig. 133, Plate 46 and Color Plate XII)

MATERIALS

468′ pink rattail; 468′ purple rattail; 620 crystal beads.

METHOD

Step 1. Measure the distance from shoulder tip to shoulder tip. Subtract 2″ from this measurement. Draw a line, this length, across the top of the knotting board.

Step 2. Cut 6 pink cords, each 9′ long. Fold the cords in half and pin, side-by-side, at the left end of the line. Cut 4 purple cords, each 9′ long. Fold the cords in half and pin, side-by-side, directly to the right of the pink cords. Beginning with the outside 4 cords on either side, tie 1 row of Square Knots. Tie 4 rows of Alternating Square Knots.

Fig. 133

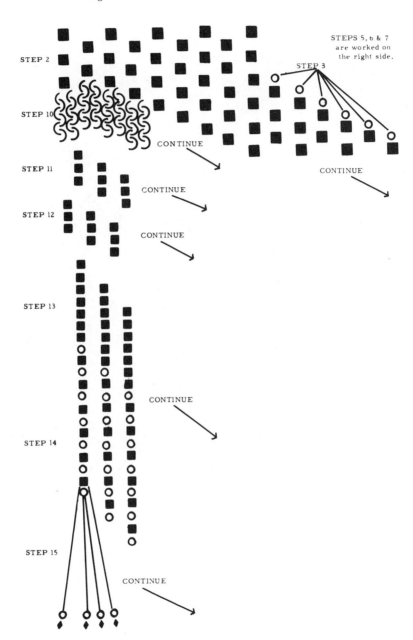

STEP 2

STEPS 5, 6 & 7
are worked on
the right side.

STEP 3

STEP 10

CONTINUE

CONTINUE

STEP 11

CONTINUE

STEP 12

CONTINUE

STEP 13

CONTINUE

STEP 14

STEP 15

CONTINUE

Plate 46. Party Tunic. Aglitter with shining rayon cord and sparkling beads, this brightly colored tunic would be a standout anywhere.

Step 3. Cut 1 purple cord 9' long. String 1 bead on the cord. Fold the cord in half, placing the bead at the fold. Pin the bead to the *right* of the last row of Alternating Square Knots. Beginning with the 4 right cords, tie 1 row of 4 Alternating Square Knots. Repeat this step eight times.

Step 4. Repeat Step 3, seven times, using *pink* cord instead of purple cord. The last bead should be just to the left of the center.

Step 5. Cut 6 pink cords, each 9' long. Fold the cords in half and pin, side-by-side, at the right end of the line. Cut 4 purple cords, each 9' long. Fold the cords in half and pin, side-by-side, directly to the left of the pink cords. Beginning with the outside 4 cords on either side, tie 1 row of Square Knots. Tie 4 rows of Alternating Square Knots.

Step 6. Cut 1 purple cord 9' long. String 1 bead on the cord. Fold the cord in half, placing the bead at the fold. Pin the bead to the *left* of the last row of Alternating Square Knots. Repeat this step eight times.

Step 7. Repeat Step 6, seven times, using *pink* cord instead of purple cord. The last bead should be just to the right of the center.

Step 8. With the 4 center cords (2 from each side), join the 2 sides together with 1 Alternating Square Knot. Tie 3 Alternating Square Knots on each side of this Alternating Square Knot.

Step 9. Directly below the knots tied in Step 8, tie 6 rows of Alternating Square Knots, *decreasing* each row by 1 Alternating Square Knot.

Step 10. Divide the cords into pairs. Tie 6 Single Chain Knots on each pair of cords.

Step 11. Leaving the first 2 cords on either side free, divide the balance of the cords into groups of 4. Tie 3 Square Knots on each group of 4 cords.

Step 12. Divide the cords into groups of 4. Tie 3 Square Knots on each group of 4 cords.

Step 13. Leaving the first 2 cords on either side free, divide the balance of the cords into groups of 4. Tie 7 Square Knots on each group of 4 cords.

Step 14. String 1 bead on each pair of core-cords. Tie 1 Square Knot below each bead. Repeat this step five more times. String 1 bead on each pair of core-cords below the last Square Knot.

Step 15. Trim all ends to 15". String 1 bead on each cord. Tie 1 Simple Overhand Knot on the end of each cord.

Step 16. Repeat Steps 1 through 15 for the back of the tunic. Sew the front and back together at the shoulder line. Place the stitches between the knots so that the thread does not show.

BEADED TUNIC

(Medium Size. See Fig. 134 and Plate 47)

MATERIALS

Heavy rayon cord in several colors; a total of 288′. Each color must be in multiples of 12′.

METHOD

Step 1. Cut 12 knotting cords, each 12′ long. Lay the centers of the cords side-by-side on the knotting board. Begin knotting in the center of the cords.

Step 2. With the 4 center cords, tie 1 Square Knot. With the 8 center cords, tie 2 Alternating Square Knots. With the 4 left cords, tie 1 Alternating Square Knot. With the 4 right cords, tie 1 Alternating Square Knot. With the 8 center cords, tie 2 Alternating Square Knots. With the 4 center cords, tie 1 Alternating Square Knot.

Step 3. Repeat Step 2, two times, leaving 1" between each of the diamond patterns formed. The center diamond pattern will be on the shoulder line.

Step 4. Repeat Steps 1, 2 and 3.

Step 5. Lay the 2 knotted portions side-by-side. With the 4 center cords (2 cords from each knotted piece) tie 1 Square Knot 5" below the last diamond patterns. This knot will join the two sides together.

Step 6. With the 8 center cords, tie 2 Alternating Square Knots. Continue tying diagonal rows of Alternating Square Knots until all cords have been tied.

Step 7. With the 4 center cords, tie 1 Square Knot 1" below the first Square Knot tied in Step 5. Directly below this knot, tie 6 rows of Alternating Square Knots, *increasing* each row by 1 Alternating Square Knot. Tie 5 rows of Alternating Square Knots, *decreasing* each row by 1 Alternating Square Knot. This will be the front of the tunic.

Step 8. Repeat Steps 5 through 7 on the back of the tunic.

Step 9. Tie 2 cords from the back and 2 cords from the front, together under the arms, with 1 Square Knot. Trim all ends to 18". String 1 bead on each cord and glue in place at random heights.

Plate 47. Beaded Tunic. For a lively addition to your wardrobe, make this quickly knotted beaded tunic. The beads are glued on and appear to float on the cords.

Fig. 134

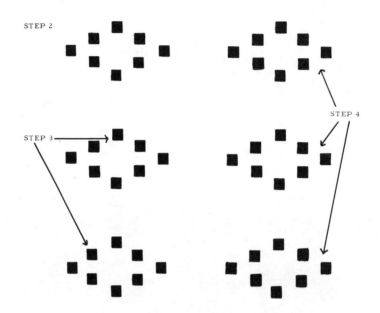

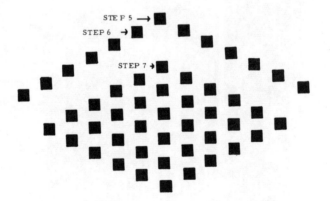

DIAMOND TUNIC

(Medium Size. See Fig. 135 and Plate 48)

MATERIALS

720′ large rayon cord

METHOD

Step 1. Measure the distance from shoulder tip to shoulder tip. Subtract 2″ from this measurement. Draw a line, this length, across the top of the knotting board. Cut 8 knotting cords, each 15′ long. Pin the centers of the cords, side-by-side, on the left end of this line with half of the cords above the line and half of the cords below the line.

Step 2. Tie 2 Square Knots. Tie 2 rows of Alternating Square Knots.

Step 3. With the 4 right cords, tie 1 Alternating Square Knot 1″ below the last row of knots.

Step 4. Cut 1 knotting cord 15′ long. Fold the cord in half and mount it on the right cord with a Clove Hitch, *just above the Alternating Square Knot tied in Step 3*. Fold these 2 new cords down beside the balance of the cords.

Step 5. Repeat Steps 1 and 2 on the right end of the line.

Step 6. With the 4 left cords, tie 1 Alternating Square Knot 1″ below the last row of knots.

Step 7. Cut 1 knotting cord 15′ long. Fold the cord in half and mount it on the left cord with a Clove Hitch, *just above the Alternating Square Knot tied in Step 6*. Fold these 2 new cords down beside the balance of the cords.

Step 8. Repeat Steps 4 through 7, seven times.

Step 9. With the 4 center cords (2 cords from each side), tie 1 Alternating Square Knot to join the two sides together.

Step 10. Beginning under the center Square Knot, and the 3rd and 7th Square Knots from the center, on each side, tie diagonal rows of Alternating Square Knots.

Step 11. Tie 1 row of Alternating Square Knots across the bottom. Trim all ends to 10″. This will complete the front of the tunic.

Step 12. Tie the same pattern of knots on the other half of the cords to form the back of the tunic.

154

Fig. 135

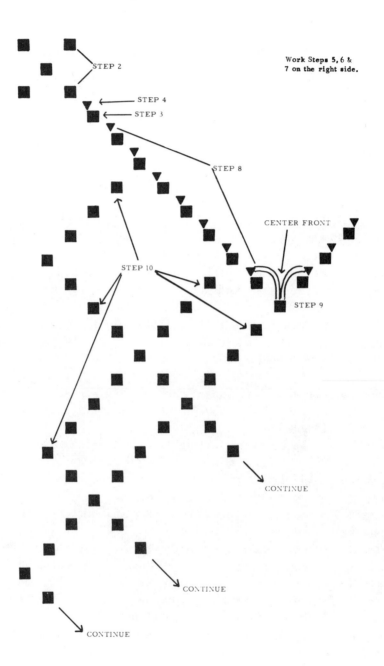

STEP 2

Work Steps **5, 6 &
7 on the right side.**

← STEP 4

← STEP 3

STEP 8

CENTER FRONT

STEP 10

STEP 9

CONTINUE

CONTINUE

CONTINUE

Plate 48. Diamond Tunic. This is a quickly knotted tunic with an airy diamond pattern that shows the contrast of the color underneath.

VEST

(Size 36. See Figs. 136, 137 and Plate 49)

MATERIALS

940′ turquoise Lily Jute-Tone; 40 large beads; 150 small beads; felt backing material.

METHOD

Step 1. Cut 8 cords, each 25′ long. Fold all the cords in half, and mount them side-by-side on the mounting board. Beginning with the outside 4 cords on either side, tie 1 row of Square Knots.

Step 2. Cut 3 cords, each 25′ long. Fold all the cords in half, and mount them side-by-side, directly to the left of the last Square Knot tied in Step 1. Beginning with the 4 left cords, tie 1 row of Alternating Square Knots.

Step 3. Tie 5 rows of Alternating Square Knots.

Step 4. With the 8 left cords, tie 2 Alternating Square Knots. With the 4 right cords, tie 1 Alternating Square Knot.

Steps 5 through 9 will form a diamond pattern of Diagonal Double Half Hitches.

Step 5. The 10th and 11th cords from the right become the *left* and *right core-cords*. The 4 cords on either side of the core-cords become the *left* and *right knotting-cords.*

Step 6. Carry the right core-cord diagonally across the right knotting-cords. Tie the right knotting-cords around the right core-cord with Diagonal Double Half Hitches.

Step 7. Carry the left core-cord diagonally across the left knotting-cords. Tie the left knotting-cords around the left core-cord with Diagonal Double Half Hitches.

Step 8. Carry the right core-cord diagonally back to the center across the right knotting-cords. Tie the right knotting-cords around the right core-cord with Diagonal Double Half Hitches.

Step 9. Carry the left core-cord diagonally back to the center across the left knotting-cords. Tie the left knotting-cords around the left core-cord with Diagonal Double Half Hitches.

Fig. 136

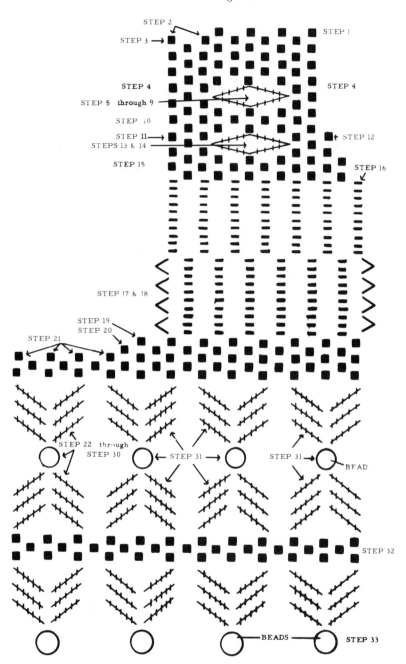

Step 10. Beginning at the outside points of the diamond, tie 5 rows of Alternating Square Knots.

Step 11. With the 8 left cords, tie 2 Alternating Square Knots.

Step 12. Cut 1 cord 25' long. Fold the cord in half, and mount it directly to the right of the last row of Alternating Square Knots. With the 8 right cords, tie 2 Alternating Square Knots.

Steps 13 and 14 will form a diamond pattern of Diagonal Double Half Hitches.

Step 13. The 12th and 13th cords from the right, become the *left* and *right core-cords*. The 4 cords on either side of the core-cords become the *left* and *right knotting-cords*.

Step 14. Repeat Steps 6 through 9.

Step 15. Repeat Step 10.

Step 16. Cut 1 cord 25' long. Fold the cord in half, and mount it directly to the right of the last row of Alternating Square Knots. Divide the cords into groups of 4. Tie 10 Half Knots on each group of 4 cords.

Step 17. With the 2 left cords, tie 4 Reversed Double Half Hitches. Repeat this step on the right.

Step 18. Divide the balance of the cords into groups of 4. Tie 10 Half Knots on each group of 4 cords.

Step 19. Cut 2 cords, each 12' long. Fold all the cords in half, and mount them side-by-side, directly to the left of the last Reversed Double Half Hitch on the left side. Beginning with the outside 4 cords on either side, tie 1 row of Square Knots.

Step 20. Cut 1 cord 12' long. Fold the cord in half, and mount it directly to the left of the last Square Knot tied in Step 19. Beginning with the 4 left cords, tie 1 row of Alternating Square Knots.

Step 21. Cut 7 cords, each 12' long. Fold all the cords in half, and mount side-by-side, directly to the left of the last row of Alternating Square Knots. Tie 3 rows of Alternating Square Knots.

Steps 22 through 30 will be worked on the 12 left cords.

Step 22. Divide the number of cords in half. The outside left cord becomes the *left core-cord*. The other 5 cords on the left become the *left knotting-cords*. The outside right cord becomes the *right core-cord*. The other 5 cords on the right become the *right knotting-cords*.

Step 23. Carry the right core-cord diagonally across the right knotting-cords. Tie the right knotting-cords around the right core-cord with Diagonal Double Half Hitches.

Step 24. Carry the left core-cord diagonally across the left knotting-cords. Tie the left knotting-cords around the left core-cord with Diagonal Double Half Hitches.

Step 25. Repeat Steps 22, 23 and 24, two more times.

Step 26. String 1 large bead on the 2 center cords.

Step 27. The 2 center cords become the *left* and *right core-cords*. The other 5 cords on the left become the *left knotting-cords*. The other 5 cords on the right become the *right knotting-cords*.

Step 28. Carry the right core-cord diagonally across the right knotting cords. Tie the right knotting-cords around the right core-cord with Diagonal Double Half Hitches.

Step 29. Carry the left core-cord diagonally across the left knotting-cords. Tie the left knotting-cords around the left core-cord with Diagonal Double Half Hitches.

Step 30. Repeat Steps 27, 28 and 29, two more times.

Step 31. Divide the balance of the cords into groups of 12. Repeat Steps 22 through 30, on each group of 12 cords.

Step 32. Beginning with the outside 4 cords on either side, tie 1 row of Square Knots. Tie 2 rows of Alternating Square Knots.

Step 33. Repeat Steps 22 through 31.

Step 34. Beginning with the outside 4 cords on either side, tie 1 row of Square Knots. Tie 6 rows of Alternating Square Knots.

Step 35. Trim all ends to 6". String large and small beads, at random, on each cord, tying 1 Simple Overhand Knot below each bead. This will complete the right front half of the vest.

Step 36. To tie the left front of the vest, repeat Steps 1 through 35, working the directions in reverse. That is, in Step 2, the 3 new cords will be added to the *right* of the last Square Knot, not to the *left*.

Plate 49. Vest. Why not surprise him with a macrame vest worked in softly textured jute and accented with large wooden beads!

Fig. 137

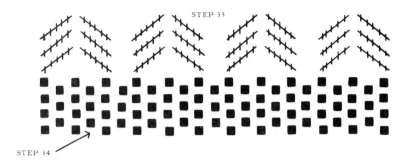

STEP 33

STEP 34

Step 37. Lay the 2 knotted pieces, face up, side-by-side with the center bottoms touching each other. Gently curve the center tops apart until they are separated by approximately 6″ at the top. Make a tracing of this outline around the top, sides and bottom for the back of the vest. Cut a felt backing to match the tracing. Sew the top and sides of the knotted pieces to the top and sides of the felt backing.

162

Fig. 138

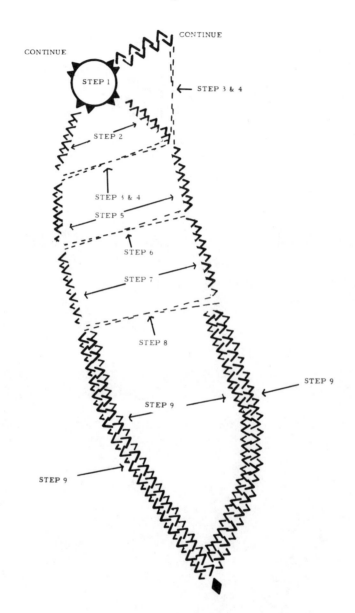

NYLON PLANT HANGER

(Accommodates 8" pot. See Fig. 138 and Plate 50)

MATERIALS

96′ nylon cord; 2″ brass or wooden ring.

METHOD

Step 1. Cut 8 cords, each 12′ long. Fold all the cords in half and mount on the ring with Clove Hitches.

Step 2. Divide the cords into groups of 4. Tie 8 Alternating Reversed Double Half Hitches on each group of 4 cords.

Step 3. Carry the left knotting-cord of one sinnet across to the core-cords of the sinnet directly to its left. Tie this knotting-cord around the new core-cords with 1 Reversed Double Half Hitch. The distance between the core-cords of the 2 sinnets should be approximately 3″. Repeat this step with all 4 sinnets.

Step 4. Carry the right knotting-cord on one sinnet across to the core-cords of the sinnet directly to its right. Tie this knotting-cord around the new core-cords with 1 Reversed Double Half Hitch. The distance between the core-cords of the 2 sinnets will be 3″ as established in Step 3.

Step 5. Repeat Step 2. Tie the 8 Alternating Reversed Double Half Hitches over the same core-cords as in Step 2.

Step 6. Repeat Steps 3 and 4. The distance between the core-cords of each sinnet should be 4½″ instead of 3″.

Step 7. Using the same core-cords as in Step 2, divide the cords into groups of 4. Tie 10 Alternating Reversed Double Half Hitches on each group of 4 cords.

Step 8. Repeat Steps 3 and 4. The distance between the core-cords of each sinnet should be 4½″.

Step 9. Divide each group of 4 cords into pairs. Tie 36 Reversed Double Half Hitches on each pair of cords. Tie all cords together with 1 Multiple-Strand Overhand Knot. Trim all ends close to knot.

Plate 50. Nylon Plant Hanger (left). Sisal Plant Hanger (center). Jute Plant Hanger (right). All three have been designed to withstand the elements. With use, they will develop their own special weathered look.

Fig. 139

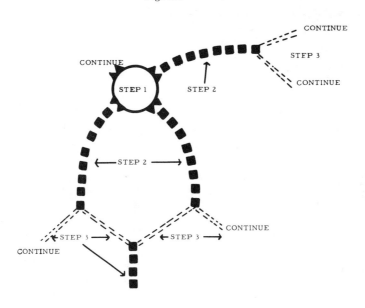

JUTE PLANT HANGER

(Accommodates 8" pot. See Fig. 139 and Plate 50)

MATERIALS

120' of two-ply jute; 2" brass or wooden ring.

METHOD

Step 1. Cut 8 cords, each 15' long. Fold all the cords in half and mount them on the ring with Clove Hitches.

Step 2. Divide the cords into groups of 4. Tie 8 Square Knots on each group of 4 cords.

Step 3. Take 2 cords from one sinnet and 2 cords from an adjoining sinnet. Leaving 1¾" between the 2 sinnets, tie 5 Square Knots with these 4 cords. Repeat this step with all the sinnets.

Step 4. Repeat Step 3, leaving 2½" between the sinnets, instead of 1¾".
Step 5. Tie 29 Double Chain Knots on each group of 4 cords.
Step 6. Tie all cords together with 1 Multiple-Strand Overhand Knot. Trim ends close to the knot.

Fig. 139

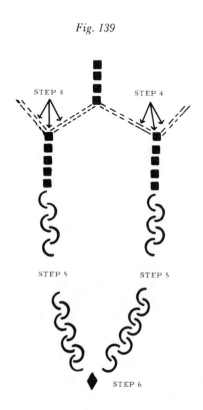

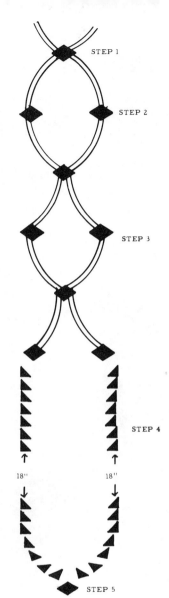

Fig. 140

STEP 1

STEP 2

STEP 3

STEP 4

18″

18″

STEP 5

SISAL PLANT HANGER

(Accomodates 7″ pot. See Fig. 140 and Plate 50)

MATERIALS

120′ sisal, ⅛″

METHOD

Step 1. Cut 8 knotting-cords, each 15′ long. Tie all the cords together with 1 Multiple-Strand Overhand Knot, 2″ from the ends of the cords.

Step 2. Divide the cords into pairs. Tie each pair of cords together with 1 Double-Strand Overhand Knot.

Step 3. Tie 4 rows of Alternating Overhand Knots 2″ apart.

Step 4. Divide the cords into pairs. Tie 18″ of Half Hitches on each pair of cords.

Step 5. Tie all the cords together with 1 Multiple-Strand Overhand Knot. Trim ends close to this knot.

Plate 51. *Striped Bookmarker (left). Diamond Pattern Bookmarker (center). Giant "X" Bookmarker (right). Ideal as bazaar or quick gift items, these are made from inexpensive cotton crochet yarn.*

DIAMOND PATTERN BOOKMARKER

(See Fig. 141 and Plate 51)

MATERIALS

16' dark rose cotton yarn; 16' medium rose cotton yarn; 8' light rose cotton yarn.

METHOD

Step 1. Cut 8 dark rose, 8 medium rose and 4 light rose cords, each 2' long. Arrange the cords on the knotting board in the following sequence: 4 dark, 4 medium, 4 light, 4 medium, 4 dark.

Step 2. Begin knotting 1½" from the point where the cords have been secured. With the 4 center cords, tie 1 Square Knot.

Step 3. Tie 4 rows of Alternating Square Knots, *increasing* each row by 1 Alternating Square Knot.

Step 4. Tie 4 rows of Alternating Square Knots, *decreasing* each row by 1 Alternating Square Knot.

Step 5. Repeat Steps 3 and 4, two times. Trim all ends to 1½ inches.

Fig. 141

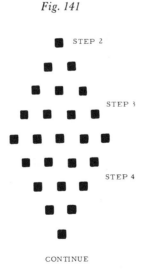

STEP 2

STEP 3

STEP 4

CONTINUE

Fig. 142

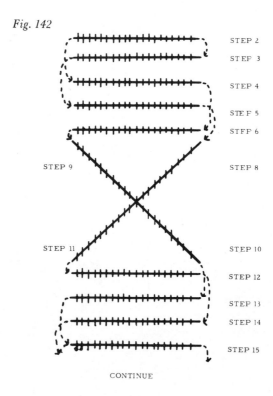

STEP 2
STEP 3
STEP 4
STEP 5
STEP 6
STEP 8
STEP 9
STEP 10
STEP 11
STEP 12
STEP 13
STEP 14
STEP 15

CONTINUE

GIANT "X" BOOKMARKER

(See Fig. 142 and Plate 51)

MATERIALS

28′ light rose cotton yarn; 20′ medium rose cotton yarn; 10′ dark rose cotton yarn.

METHOD

Step 1. Cut 1 light rose core-cord 1½′ long. Cut 8 light rose, 8 medium rose, and 4 dark rose knotting-cords, each 2½′ long. Arrange the knotting-cords on the knotting board in the following sequence: 4 light rose, 4 medium rose, 4 dark rose, 4 medium rose, 4 light rose.

Step 2. Lay the center of the core-cord horizontally across all the knotting-cords, 1¾″ from the point where the cords have been secured. Tie all the knotting-cords around the center of the core-cord with Horizontal Double Half Hitches. The right end of the core-cord becomes the *right core-cord*. The left end of the core-cord becomes the *left core-cord*.

Step 3. Carry the right core-cord horizontally across all the knotting-cords directly below the last row of knots. Tie all the knotting cords around the right core-cord with Horizontal Double Half Hitches.

Step 4. Carry the left core-cord horizontally across all the knotting-cords directly below the last row of knots. Tie all the knotting-cords around the left core-cord with Horizontal Double Half Hitches.

Step 5. Carry the right core-cord (presently on the left side) horizontally across all the knotting-cords directly below the last row of knots. Tie all the knotting-cords around the right core-cord with Horizontal Double Half Hitches.

Step 6. Carry the left core-cord (presently on the right side) horizontally across all the knotting-cords directly below the last row of knots. Tie all the knotting-cords around the left core-cord with Horizontal Double Half Hitches.

Steps 7 through 11 will form an "X" pattern of Diagonal Double Half Hitches.

Step 7. Divide the number of cords in half. The outside left cord becomes the *left core-cord*. The other 10 cords on the left become the *left knotting-cords*. The outside right cord becomes the *right core-cord*. The other 10 cords on the right become the *right knotting-cords*.

Step 8. Carry the right core-cord diagonally across the right knotting-cords. Tie the right knotting-cords around the right core-cord with Diagonal Double Half Hitches.

Step 9. Carry the left core-cord diagonally across the left knotting-cords. Tie the left knotting-cords around the left core-cord with Diagonal Double Half Hitches.

Step 10. Cross the left core-cord over the right core-cord and carry it diagonally over the right knotting-cords. Tie the right knotting-cords around the left core-cord with Diagonal Double Half Hitches.

Step 11. Take the right core-cord, which lies under the left core-cord, and carry it diagonally *over* the left knotting-cords. Tie the left knotting-cords around the right core-cord with Diagonal Double Half Hitches.

Step 12. Carry the right core-cord (presently on the left side) horizontally across all the knotting-cords. Tie all the knotting-cords around the right core-cord with Horizontal Double Half Hitches.

Step 13. Carry the left core-cord (presently on the right side) horizontally across all the knotting cords directly below the last row of knots. Tie all the knotting-cords around the left core-cord with Horizontal Double Half Hitches.

Step 14. Carry the right core-cord horizontally across all the knotting-cords directly below the last row of knots. Tie all the knotting-cords around the right core-cord with Horizontal Double Half Hitches.

Step 15. Carry the left core-cord horizontally across all the knotting-cords directly below the last row of knots. Tie all the knotting cords around the left core-cord with Horizontal Double Half Hitches.

Step 16. Repeat Steps 7 through 15. Trim all ends to 1¾".

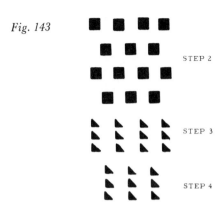

Fig. 143

STEP 2

STEP 3

STEP 4

CONTINUE

STRIPED BOOKMARKER

(See Fig. 143 and Plate 51)

MATERIALS

20′ dark rose cotton yarn; 20′ light rose cotton yarn.

METHOD

Step 1. Cut 8 dark rose and 8 light rose cords, each 2½′ long. Arrange the cords on the knotting board in the following sequence: 4 dark, 4 light, 4 dark, 4 light.

Step 2. Begin knotting 1½″ from the point where the cords have been secured. Beginning with the outside 4 cords on either side, tie 1 row of Square Knots. Tie 3 rows of Alternating Square Knots.

Step 3. Divide the cords into groups of 4. Tie 3 Half Hitches, over 3 core-cords, on each group of 4 cords.

Step 4. Leaving the first 2 cords on either side free, divide the balance of the cords into groups of 4. Tie 3 Half Hitches, over 3 core-cords, on each group of 4 cords.

Step 5. Repeat the above steps in the following sequence: 3, 4, 2, 3, 4, 5, 2. Trim all ends to 1½″.

BEADED BOTTLE COVER

(See Figs. 144, 145, Plate 52 and Color Plate III)

MATERIALS

Large Glass Bottle, approximately 11″ in diameter and 2′ tall; 360′ dark gold rug yarn; 360′ light gold rug yarn; 48 red barrel beads; 154 square blue beads.

METHOD

Step 1. Cut 1 light gold holding-cord 18″ long. Cut 12 dark gold and 12 light gold knotting-cords, each 15′ long. Fold all the knotting-cords in half and mount them with Clove Hitches on the holding-cord in the following sequence: 6 light gold, 6 dark gold, 6 light gold, 6 dark gold.

Step 2. Tie the holding-cord around the neck of the bottle. Wrap the ends of the holding-cord around the neck of the bottle under the knotting-cords several times. Glue the ends in place. Divide the cords into groups of 4, keeping the light and dark cords separate. Tie 1 row of Square Knots. Tie 5 rows of Alternating Square Knots. The knots should be allowed to spread naturally over the surface of the bottle.

Step 3. Tie the top half of 1 row of Alternating Square Knots. String 1 red barrel bead on each pair of core-cords. Tie the bottom half of the Alternating Square Knot, directly below each bead. The knotting cords for each Alternating Square Knot will pass around the sides of each bead. Repeat this step, three more times.

Step 4. Cut 1 dark gold core-cord 3′ long. String 12 blue beads on this core-cord. Lay this core-cord around the bottle, over all the knotting-cords, directly below the last row of Alternating Square Knots. Position 1 blue bead between each of the Alternating Square Knots. Tie all the cords around this core-cord with 1 row of Horizontal Double Half Hitches. Tie the ends of the core-cord together and slip this knot behind some of the other knots.

Fig. 144

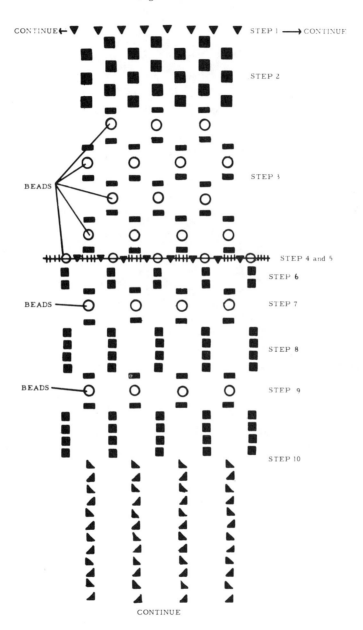

Fig. 145

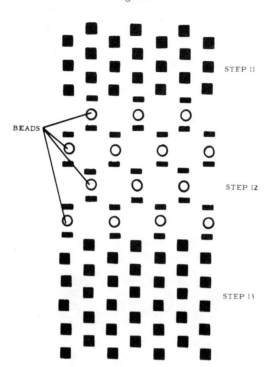

BEADS

STEP 11

STEP 12

STEP 13

Step 5. Cut 12 dark gold and 12 light gold knotting-cords, each 15′ long. Fold all the knotting-cords in half and mount them with Clove Hitches on the core-cord, placing 1 knotting-cord on each side of each of the blue beads.

Step 6. With 4 of these new knotting-cords, tie 2 Square Knots. Divide the balance of the cords into groups of 4. Tie 2 Square Knots on each group of 4 cords.

Step 7. Tie the top half of 1 row of Alternating Square Knots. String 1 square blue bead on each pair of core-cords. Tie the bottom half of the Alternating Square Knot directly below each bead. The knotting-cords for each Alternating Square Knot will pass around the sides of each bead.

Step 8. Tie 1 row of Alternating Square Knots. Tie 3 more Square Knots directly below each of these Alternating Square Knots.

Step 9. Repeat Steps 7 and 8.

Step 10. With 2 cords from each Square Knot, tie 12 Alternating Half Hitches over a double core.

Step 11. Tie 6 rows of Alternating Square Knots.

Step 12. Repeat Step 7, four times.

Step 13. Tie 10 rows of Alternating Square Knots. These knots will carry the cords under the bottom of the bottle. Gradually increase the tension on the cords. Trim the cords below the last row of knots and glue in place.

Plate 52. Jute Bottle Cover (left). Beaded Bottle Cover (center). Rayon Bottle Cover (right). For an eye-stopping conversation piece, cover a bottle with macrame! These bottles range in size from ½ gallon capacity up to a giant water cooler size.

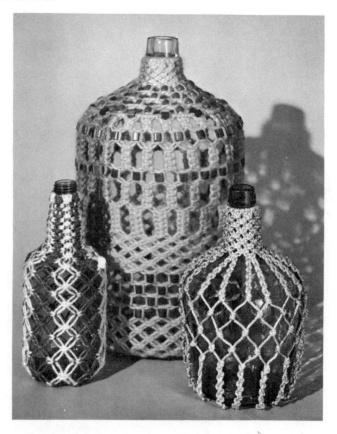

JUTE BOTTLE COVER

(See Fig. 146, Plate 52 and Color Plate III)

MATERIALS

½ gallon wine bottle; 64' white Lily Jute-Tone; 65' red Lily Jute-Tone.

METHOD

Step 1. Cut 1 red holding-cord 12" long. Cut 8 red and 8 white knotting-cords, each 8' long. Fold all the knotting-cords in half and mount them on the holding-cord with Clove Hitches in the following sequence: 2 white, 2 red, 2 white, 2 red, 2 white, 2 red, 2 white, 2 red.

Step 2. Tie the holding-cord around the neck of the bottle. Wrap the ends of the holding-cord around the neck of the bottle under the knotting-cords several times. Glue the ends.

Step 3. Divide the cords into groups of 4, keeping the red and white cords separate. Tie 1 row of Square Knots. Tie rows of Alternating Square Knots until the entire bottle is covered. Relax the tension on the cords as the knotting progresses over the bulge of the bottle. Gradually increase the tension on the cords as the knotting progresses under the bottle. Knot to the center of the bottom of the bottle. Trim all ends close to the last row of knots and glue in place.

Fig. 146

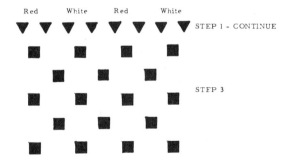

RAYON BOTTLE COVER

(See Fig. 147, Plate 52 and Color Plate III)

MATERIALS

1 gallon wine bottle; 25′ gold rayon cord; 24′ blue rayon cord.

METHOD

Step 1. Cut 1 gold holding-cord 12″ long. Cut 8 gold and 8 blue knotting-cords, each 3′ long. Fold all the knotting-cords in half and mount them on the holding-cord with Clove Hitches in the following sequence: 4 gold, 4 blue, 4 gold, 4 blue.

Step 2. Tie the holding-cord around the neck of the bottle. Wrap the ends of the holding-cord around the neck of the bottle under the knotting cords several times. Glue the ends in place. Divide the cords into groups of 4, keeping the blue and yellow cords separate. Tie 1 row of Square Knots. Tie 7 rows of Alternating Square Knots.

Step 3. Divide the cords into pairs, keeping the blue and yellow cords separate. Tie 10 Single Chain Knots on each pair of cords.

Step 4. Tie 1 Double-Strand Overhand Knot below the last Single Chain Knot. Tie 4 rows of Alternating Overhand Knots.

Step 5. Divide the cords into pairs, keeping the blue and yellow cords separate. Tie 15 Single Chain Knots on each pair of cords. These knots will carry the cords under the bottom of the bottle.

Step 6. Divide the cords into groups of 4, still keeping the blue and yellow cords separate. Tie 1 Square Knot on each group of 4 cords. Tie 4 rows of Alternating Square Knots. Gradually increase the tension on the cords to pull the knots toward the center of the bottom. Trim the cords below the last row and glue in place.

Fig. 147

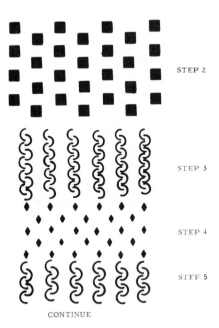

STEP 2

STEP 3

STEP 4

STEP 5

CONTINUE

SQUARE KNOT PILLOW TOP

(See Fig. 148, Plate 53 and Color Plate II)

MATERIALS

294' red rug yarn; 9½" by 14" pillow form.

METHOD

Step 1. Cut 1 holding-cord 18" long. Cut 44 knotting-cords, each 6' long. Lay all the knotting-cords on the knotting board, side-by-side. Lay the holding-cord across all the knotting-cords, 1½" from the point where the cords have been secured. Tie all the knotting-cords around the holding-cord with Horizontal Double Half Hitches. This will make a fringe at one end of the pillow top.

Step 2. Divide the cords into groups of 4. Tie 3 Square Knots on each group of 4 cords.

Step 3. Leaving the 2 outside cords on each side free, divide the remaining cords into groups of 4. Tie 3 Square Knots on each group of 4 cords.

Step 4. Repeat Step 2.

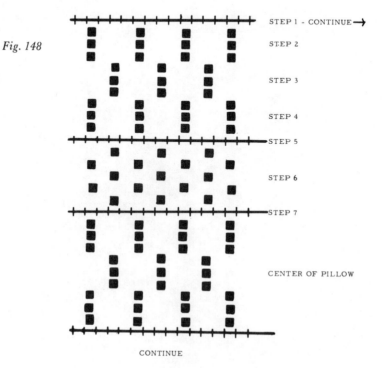

Fig. 148

STEP 1 - CONTINUE →
STEP 2
STEP 3
STEP 4
STEP 5
STEP 6
STEP 7

CENTER OF PILLOW

CONTINUE

Step 5. Cut 1 core-cord 18″ long. Lay the core-cord across all the knotting-cords directly below the last row of Square Knots. Tie all the knotting-cords around the core-cord with Horizontal Double Half Hitches.

Step 6. Beginning with the outside 4 cords on either side, tie 1 row of Square Knots. Tie 4 rows of Alternating Square Knots.

Step 7. Repeat the above steps in the following sequence: 5, 2 through 7, 2 through 5. Trim all ends to 1½″ to form the fringe at the other end of the pillow.

Step 8. Sew the edge of the knotted piece to the top edge of a pillow form. Place stitches between the knots so that the thread does not show.

Plate 53. Square Knot Pillow (top). Diamond Pillow (bottom). Made with rug yarn, these open patterns allow for an interesting play of colors between the knotted design and the fabric behind the cords. Diamond Pillow Courtesy Abbey Sperber.

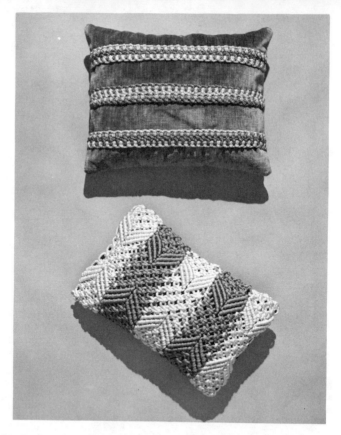

Plate 54. Braided Pillow (top). Rayon Chevron Pillow (bottom). The Braided Pillow has three stripes of rayon braid appliquéd to the top of a velvet pillow. The Rayon Chevron Pillow contrasts the chevron design against the plainer pattern of flat Alternating Square Knots.

BRAIDED PILLOW TOP

(See Fig. 149, Plate 54 and Color Plate II)

The following materials and instructions will produce 1 braid 15″ long.

MATERIALS

24′ yellow rayon cord; 16′ blue rayon cord; 11″ by 14″ pillow.

METHOD

Step 1. Cut 4 yellow core-cords, each 2′ long. Cut 2 yellow knotting-cords, each 8′ long. Cut 2 blue knotting-cords, each 8′ long. Arrange the cords on the knotting board in the following sequence: 1 yellow knotting-cord, 2 yellow core-cords, 2 blue knotting-cords, 2 yellow core-cords, 1 yellow knotting-cord. Leave ½" between the 2 blue knotting cords. Number the cords from left to right. The knotting-cords will be tied with Reversed Double Half Hitches over 2 core-cords.

Step 2. Tie knotting-cord 1 over core-cords 2 and 3.

Step 3. Tie knotting-cord 8 over core-cords 6 and 7.

Step 4. Tie knotting-cord 4 over core-cords 6 and 7.

Step 5. Cross knotting-cord 5 over knotting-cord 4 and tie it over core-cords 2 and 3.

Step 6. Repeat Steps 2 and 3.

Step 7. Tie knotting-cord 5 over core-cords 6 and 7.

Step 8. Cross knotting-cord 4 over knotting-cord 5 and tie it over core-cords 2 and 3.

Step 9. Continue tying this sequence of knots until the desired length is reached.

Step 10. Tie a 2nd braid following the same color placement.

Step 11. Tie a 3rd braid *reversing the color placement of the knotting-cords.*

Step 12. Sew the braid to the face of a pillow, alternating the colors of braid. Place the stitches between the knots so that the thread does not show.

Fig. 149

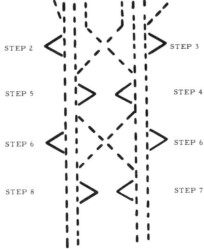

CHEVRON PILLOW TOP

(See Fig. 150, Plate 54 and Color Plate II)

MATERIALS

54′ large pink rayon cord; 36′ large blue rayon cord; 9″ by 14″ pillow form.

METHOD

Step 1. Cut 18 pink and 12 blue cords, each 3′ long. Fold all the knotting-cords in half and mount them on the knotting board in the following sequence: 6 pink, 6 blue, 6 pink, 6 blue, 6 pink.

Step 2. Beginning with the outside 4 cords on either side, tie 1 row of Square Knots. Tie 2 rows of Alternating Square Knots.

Step 3. Divide the cords into groups, according to color. With the 8 center cords of each color group, tie 2 Alternating Square Knots. With the 4 center cords of each color group, tie 1 Alternating Square Knot.
Steps 4 through 7 will be tied on the center group of pink cords.

Step 4. Divide the number of cords in half. The outside left cord becomes the *left core-cord*. The other 5 cords on the left become the *left knotting-cords*. The outside right cord becomes the *right core-cord*. The other 5 cords on the right become the *right knotting-cords*.

Step 5. Carry the right core-cord diagonally across the right knotting-cords. Tie the right knotting-cords around the right core-cord with Diagonal Double Half Hitches.

Step 6. Carry the left core-cord diagonally across the left knotting-cords. Tie the left knotting-cords around the left core-cord with Diagonal Double Half Hitches.

Step 7. Repeat Steps 4, 5 and 6, two times.

Step 8. Divide the balance of the cords into groups, according to color. Repeat Steps 4 through 7 for each color group.

Step 9. With 2 cords from each color group, that is, 2 pink and 2 blue, tie 1 Square Knot.

Step 10. Tie 2 Alternating Square Knots directly below the Square Knot tied in Step 9.

Step 11. With the 4 left cords, tie 1 Square Knot. Repeat this step on the right.

Step 12. Leaving the 2 outside cords on each side free, tie 1 row of Alternating Square Knots. Tie 4 more rows of Alternating Square Knots.

Step 13. Repeat the above steps in the following sequence: 11, 10, 9. *Steps 14 through 16 will be tied on the center group of pink cords.*

Fig. 150

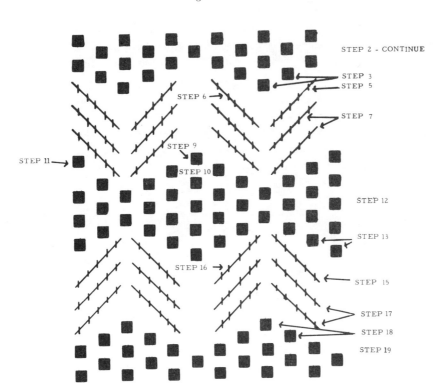

Step 14. The 2 center cords become the *left* and *right core-cords*. The other 5 cords on the left become the *left knotting-cords*. The other 5 cords on the right become the *right knotting-cords*.

Step 15. Carry the right core-cord diagonally across the right knotting-cords. Tie the right knotting-cord around the right core-cord with Diagonal Double Half Hitches.

Step 16. Carry the left core-cord diagonally across the left knotting-cords. Tie the left knotting-cords around the left core-cord with Diagonal Double Half Hitches.

Step 17. Repeat Steps 14, 15 and 16, two times.

Step 18. Divide the cords into groups, according to color. With the 4 center cords of each color group, tie 1 Square Knot. With the 8 center cords of each color group, tie 2 Alternating Square Knots.

Step 19. Beginning with the outside 4 cords on either side, tie 1 row of Alternating Square Knots. Tie 2 more rows of Alternating Square Knots.

Step 20. Carry all the cords to the reverse side and thread them through the back of several knots. Trim all the ends close to the back of the piece and glue down. Sew the sides of the chevron pattern together, on the reverse side. Sew the edge of the knotted piece to the top edge of a pillow form. Place stitches between the knots so that the thread does not show.

DIAMOND PILLOW TOP

(See Fig. 151 and Plate 53)

MATERIALS

106' rug yarn; 12" square pillow form.

METHOD

Step 1. Cut 1 holding-cord 2' long. Cut 26 knotting-cords, each 4' long. Fold all the knotting-cords in half and mount them on the holding-cord with Clove Hitches.

Step 2. Divide the cords into groups of 4. Tie 3 Square Knots on each group of 4 cords.

Step 3. With the 3rd, 4th, 5th and 6th cords from the left, tie 3 Square Knots. Repeat this step on the right.

Fig. 151

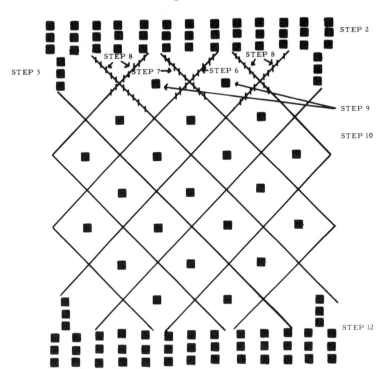

Step 4. Divide the balance of the cords into groups of 12. *Steps 5 through 7 will be worked on the center group of 12 cords.*

Step 5. Divide the number of cords in half. The outside left cord becomes the *left core-cord.* The other 5 cords on the left become the *left knotting-cords.* The outside right cord becomes the *right core-cord.* The other 5 cords on the right become the *right knotting-cords.*

Step 6. Carry the right core-cord diagonally across the right knotting-cords. Tie the right knotting-cords around the right core-cord with Diagonal Double Half Hitches.

Step 7. Carry the left core-cord diagonally across the left knotting-cords. Tie the left knotting-cords around the left core-cord with Diagonal Double Half Hitches.

Step 8. Repeat Steps 5, 6 and 7 on the other 2 groups of 12 cords.

Step 9. With 2 cords from adjoining groups of cords, tie 1 Square Knot even with the bottom of the "V" formed by Steps 4 through 7.

Step 10. Cross the core-cords over each other and continue tying rows of Diagonal Double Half Hitches. Tie 1 Square Knot in the center of each diamond pattern. When a core-cord reaches the outside edge of the knotted piece, carry it diagonally back across the cords to continue the diamond pattern.

Step 11. Tie 3 complete diamond patterns down the center of the pillow. Tie ½ of a diamond pattern at the bottom of the pillow.

Step 12. Repeat Step 3, followed by Step 2.

Step 13. Carry all the cords to the reverse side and thread them through the back of several knots. Trim all the ends close to the back of the piece and glue in place. Sew the edge of the knotted piece to the top edge of a pillow form. Place stitches between the knots so that the thread does not show.

Plate 55. Room Divider. This large room divider could be expanded, either horizontally or vertically. The simple patterns of knots are accented with brightly colored beads.

ROOM DIVIDER

(36" by 48". See Fig. 152, Plate 55 and Color Plate VII)

MATERIALS

432' red Lily Jute-Tone; 432' white Lily Jute-Tone; 336 large beads; 2 wooden dowels, ¾ diameter, 36" long.

METHOD

Step 1. Cut 24 red and 24 white cords, each 18' long. Fold all the cords in half and string 1 bead over the fold of each cord. Slide the bead 12" down from the fold. Mount all the cords on one of the dowels with Clove Hitches in the following sequence: 6 red, 12 white, 12 red, 12 white, 6 red. Slide each bead up to the bottom of the Clove Hitches.

Step 2. Beginning with the outside 4 cords on either side, tie 1 row of Square Knots.

Step 3. Leaving the 3 outside cords on each side free, divide the balance of the cords into pairs. Beginning with the outside pair of cords on either side, string 1 bead on *every other pair of cords*. Tie 1 Square Knot below each bead. Repeat this step, one more time.

Step 4. Divide the cords into groups of 4. Tie 3 Square Knots on each group of 4 cords.

Step 5. Leaving the first 2 cords on either side free, divide the balance of the cords into groups of 4. Tie 9 Square Knots on each group of 4 cords.

Step 6. Repeat Step 4.

Step 7. Leaving 2 outside cords on each side free, tie 1 row Square Knots.

Step 8. Repeat Step 3, using 4 instead of 3 beads.

Step 9. Repeat Step 4.

Step 10. With 2 left cords, tie 28 Half Hitches. Repeat step on right.

Step 11. With the 4 center cords, tie 14 Square Knots. Divide the balance of the cords into groups of 4. Tie 28 Half Knots on each group of 4 cords.

Step 12. Beginning with the outside 4 cords on either side, tie 1 row of Square Knots. Tie 4 rows of Alternating Square Knots, leaving 1½" between each row.

Step 13. Repeat Steps 3 through 12, in *reverse* order.

Step 14. Divide the cords into groups of 4. Carry 2 cords of each group of 4 cords behind the second dowel. Carry the other 2 cords of each group of 4 cords in front of the dowel. Tie each group of 4 cords together under the dowel with 1 Multiple-Strand Overhand Knot. Trim all ends to 3½".

Fig. 152

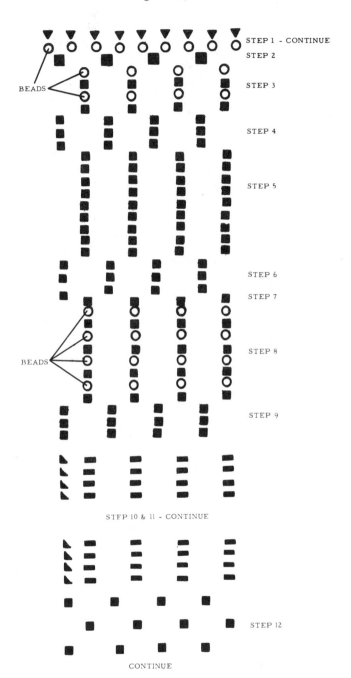

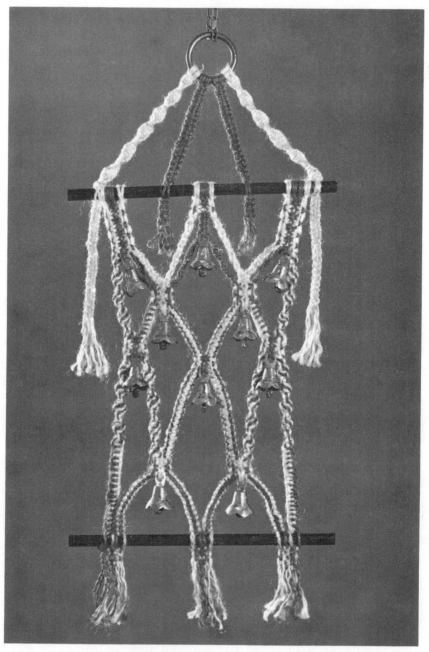

Plate 56. Bells of India Wall Hanging. Part of the enjoyment of macramé comes from combining other decorative materials with the cords; in this case, the small Indian bells are a delightful touch.

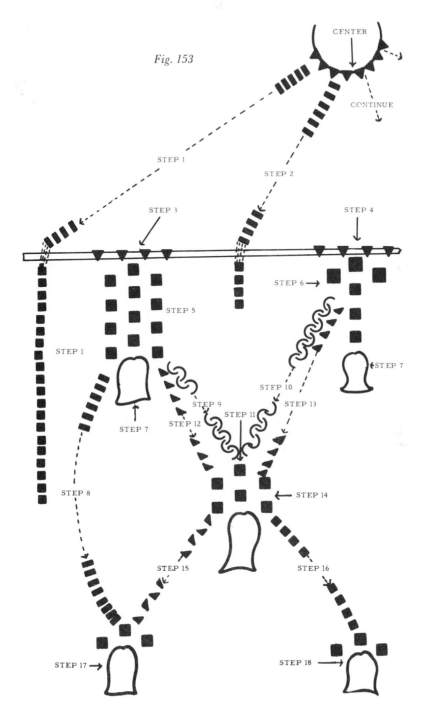

Fig. 153

BELLS OF INDIA

(12" by 26". See Figs. 153, 154 and Plate 56)

MATERIALS

90' white Lily Jute-Tone; 78' Lily Jute-Tone; 2¼" brass ring; 2 wooden dowels, 12" long; 10 brass bells, approximately 1¼" high.

METHOD

Step 1. Cut 2 white cords, each 9' long. Fold the cords in half and mount them on the brass ring with Clove Hitches. Tie 52 Half Knots. Carry the core-cords behind the wooden dowel and the knotting-cords in front of the wooden dowel, 1" from the left end of the wooden dowel. Tie 20 Square Knots below the wooden dowel. Trim the ends of the cords to 2¾". Repeat this step on the right.

Step 2. Cut 2 red cords, each 6' long. Fold the cords in half and mount them on the brass ring with Clove Hitches, between the 2 groups of white cords. Tie 18 Square Knots. Carry the core-cords behind the wooden dowel and the knotting-cords in front of the wooden dowel, 3½" from the left end of the wooden dowel. Tie 4 Square Knots below the wooden dowel. Trim the ends of the cords to 2¾". Repeat this step on the right.

Step 3. Cut 2 white and 2 red cords, each 9' long. Fold the cords in half and mount them 1¾" from the left end of the wooden dowel with Clove Hitches in the following sequence: 1 white, 2 red, 1 white. Repeat this step on the right.

Step 4. Cut 2 white and 2 red cords, each 9' long. Fold the cords in half and mount them in the center of the wooden dowel with Clove Hitches in the following sequence: 1 white, 2 red, 1 white.

Step 5. With the 4 center cords from the left and right group of cords, tie 1 Square Knot. Tie 7 rows of Alternating Square Knots on the left and right groups of cords.

Step 6. With the 4 center cords from the center group of cords, tie 1 Square Knot. With the center group of cords, tie 2 Alternating Square Knots. With the 4 center cords from the center group of cords, tie 3 Square Knots.

Step 7. String 1 bell on the 2 center cords of each group of cords.

Step 8. With the 4 left cords, tie 30 Half Knots. Repeat this step on the right.

Step 9. With the unknotted white cords from the left and right group of cords, tie 10 Single Chain Knots.

Step 10. With the white cords from the center group of cords, tie 13 Single Chain Knots.

Step 11. Join the 2 white cords from the side groups to the 2 white cords from the center group with 1 Square Knot.

Step 12. With the unknotted red cords from the left and right group of cords, tie 15 Half Hitches.

Fig. 154

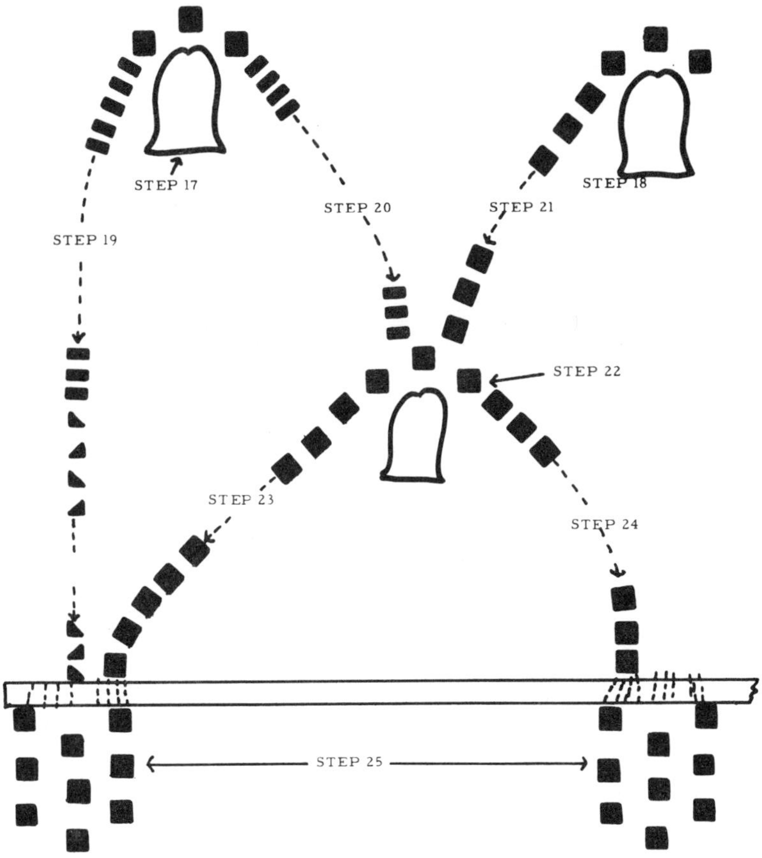

STEP 17 STEP 18 STEP 19 STEP 20 STEP 21 STEP 22 STEP 23 STEP 24 STEP 25

Step 13. With the unknotted red cords from the center group of cords, tie 16 Half Hitches.

Step 14. With the cords used in Steps 11, 12 and 13, tie 3 rows of Alternating Square Knots. String 1 bell on the 2 center cords below the last row of Alternating Square Knots.

Step 15. With the 4 cords on the outside of the bell, tie 15 Alternating Half Hitches.

Step 16. With the 4 cords on the inside of the bell, tie 10 Square Knots.

Step 17. Join the 8 left cords together with 2 rows of Alternating Square Knots. String 1 bell on the 2 center cords below the last row of Alternating Square Knots. Repeat this step on the right.

Step 18. Join the 8 center cords together with 2 rows of Alternating Square Knots. String 1 bell on the 2 center cords below the last row of Alternating Square Knots.

Step 19. With the 4 left cords, tie 30 Half Knots, followed by 35 Alternating Half Hitches. Repeat this step on the right.

Step 20. With the 5th, 6th, 7th and 8th cords from the left, tie 30 Half Knots. Repeat this step on the right.

Step 21. Divide the 8 center cords into 2 groups of 4 cords. Tie 15 Square Knots on each group of 4 cords.

Step 22. With the cords used in Steps 20 and 21, tie 3 rows of Alternating Square Knots. String 1 bell on the 2 center cords below the last row of Alternating Square Knots.

Step 23. With the 4 cords on the outside of the bell, tie 14 Square Knots.

Step 24. With the 4 cords on the inside of the bell, tie 14 Square Knots.

Step 25. Divide the 8 left cords into pairs. Carry 2 pair of cords behind the second wooden dowel and 2 pair of cords in front of the wooden dowel. With the 8 left cords, tie 6 rows of Alternating Square Knots. Repeat this step with the 8 right cords and the 8 center cords. Trim all ends to 3".

SISAL AND SHELL WALL HANGING

(15" by 30". See Figs. 155-157, Plate 57 and Color Plate X)

MATERIALS

420' of ⅛" sisal; 20 shells; 8 small screw hooks; 15" wooden molding. This hanging was worked in natural sisal *(See Plate 57)* and subsequently the side sections were dyed orange and the center section, brown/orange *(See Color Plate X)*.

Plate 57. Sisal and Shell Wall Hanging. Natural sisal makes this a good decoration for patio or terrace. Each section was dyed, after knotting, to produce a harmonious composition.

METHOD

CENTER SECTION *(See Figs. 155, 156)*

Step 1. Cut 1 holding-cord 15′ long. Cut 8 knotting-cords, each 15′ long. Fold all the knotting-cords in half and mount them on the center of the holding-cord with Clove Hitches. Fold the ends of the holding-cords down beside the knotting-cords.

Step 2. Divide the number of cords in half. The outside left cord becomes the *left core-cord*. The other 8 cords on the left become the *left knotting-cords*. The outside right cord becomes the *right core-cord*. The other 8 cords on the right become the *right knotting-cords*.

Step 3. Carry the right core-cord diagonally across the right knotting-cords. Tie the right knotting-cords around the right core-cord with Diagonal Double Half Hitches.

Step 4. Carry the left core-cord diagonally across the left knotting-cords. Tie the left knotting-cords around the left core-cord with Diagonal Double Half Hitches.

Step 5. With the 2 center cords, tie 8 Single Chain Knots.

Step 6. With the 4 left cords, tie 8 Square Knots. Repeat this step on the right.

Step 7. With the 4 unknotted cords on the left, tie 6 Square Knots. Repeat this step on the right.

Step 8. The 2 center cords become the *left* and *right core-cords*. The other 8 cords on the left become the *left knotting-cords*. The other 8 cords on the right become the *right knotting-cords*.

Step 9. Carry the right core-cord horizontally across the right knotting-cords. Tie the right knotting-cords around the right core-cord with Horizontal Double Half Hitches.

Step 10. Carry the left core-cord horizontally across the left knotting-cords. Tie the left knotting-cords around the left core-cord with Horizontal Double Half Hitches.

Step 11. Tie 1 Single Overhand Knot on each of the core-cords at the outside of the piece.

Step 12. Carry the right core-cord horizontally back to the center across the right knotting-cords. Tie the right knotting-cords around the right core-cord with Horizontal Double Half Hitches.

Step 13. Carry the left core-cord horizontally back to the center across the left knotting-cords. Tie the left knotting-cords around the left core-cord with Horizontal Double Half Hitches.

Step 14. Tie 1 Simple Overhand Knot on each of the core-cords between the 2 center cords.

Step 15. Repeat the above steps in the following sequence: 9 through 14, 9, 10.

Step 16. With the 2 center cords, tie 5 Alternating Double Half Hitches. Divide the balance of the cords in pairs. Tie 16 Half Hitches on each pair of cords.

Step 17. With the 3 left cords, tie 1 Square Knot. This Square Knot will be tied over only 1 core-cord. Repeat this step on the right.

Step 18. Divide the balance of the cords into groups of 4. Tie 1 Square Knot on each group of 4 cords.

Step 19. Tie 4 rows of Alternating Square Knots. The Square Knots on the outside of the 2nd and 4th rows will be tied over only 1 core-cord. *Steps 20, 21 and 22 will form an "X" pattern of Diagonal Double Half Hitches.*

Step 20. Repeat Steps 2, 3 and 4.

Step 21. Cross the left core-cord over the right core-cord and carry it diagonally over the right knotting-cords. Tie the right knotting-cords around the left core-cord with Diagonal Double Half Hitches.

Step 22. Take the right core-cord, which lies under the left core-cord, and carry it diagonally *over* the left knotting-cords. Tie the left knotting-cords around the right core-cord with Diagonal Double Half Hitches.

Step 23. With the 4 center cords, tie 16 Square Knots. Tie 2 Double-Strand Overhand Knots below the last Square Knot.

Step 24. With the 3rd, 4th, 5th and 6th cords from the left, tie 9 Square Knots. Tie 1 Multiple-Strand Overhand Knot below the last Square Knot. Repeat this step on the right.

Step 25. With the 2 left cords, tie 11 Half Hitches. Tie 1 Double-Strand Overhand Knot below the last Half Hitch. Repeat this step on the right.

Step 26. With the 2 unknotted cords on the left, tie 18 Half Hitches. Tie 1 Double-Strand Overhand Knot below the last Half Hitch. Repeat this step on the right.

Step 27. Trim all ends to 5″ and untwist cords to form tassels.

202

Fig. 155

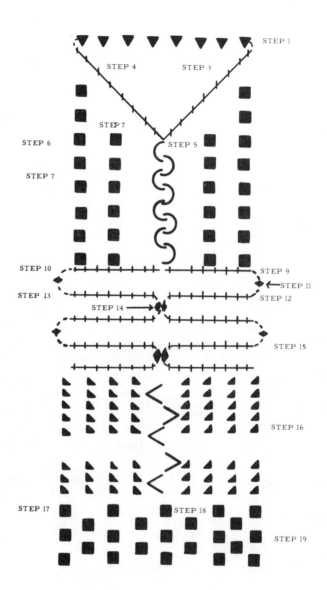

Fig. 156   203

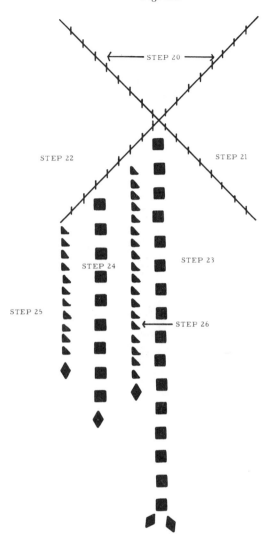

SIDE SECTION *(See Fig. 157)*

(It will be necessary to tie 2 side sections.)

Step 28. Cut 1 holding-cord 15′ long. Cut 5 knotting-cords, each 15′ long. Fold all the knotting-cords in half and mount them on the center of the holding-cord with Clove Hitches. Fold the ends of the holding-cords down beside the knotting-cords.

Fig. 157

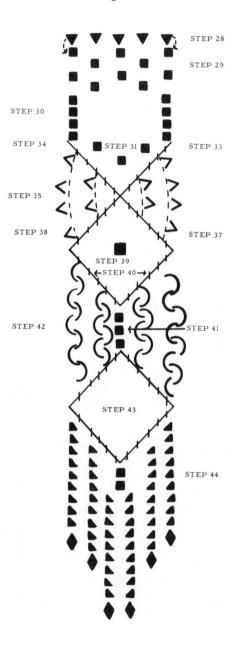

STEP 28

STEP 29

STEP 30

STEP 34   STEP 31   STEP 33

STEP 35

STEP 38   STEP 37

STEP 39

←STEP 40→

STEP 42   STEP 41

STEP 43

STEP 44

Step 29. Beginning with the outside 4 cords on either side, tie 1 row of Square Knots. Tie 3 rows of Alternating Square Knots.

Step 30. With the 4 left cords, tie 4 Square Knots. Repeat this step on the right.

Step 31. With the 8 center cords, tie 1 row of 2 Square Knots. With the 4 center cords, tie 1 Square Knot.

Step 32. Divide the number of cords in half. The outside left cord becomes the *left core-cord*. The other 5 cords on the left become the *left knotting-cords*. The outside right cord becomes the *right core-cord*. The other 5 cords on the right become the *right knotting-cords*.

Step 33. Carry the right core-cord diagonally across the right knotting-cords. Tie the right knotting-cords around the right core-cord.

Step 34. Carry the left core-cord diagonally across the left knotting-cords. Tie the left knotting-cords around the left core-cord.

Step 35. With the 2 left cords, tie 4 Reversed Double Half Hitches. The outside cord becomes the knotting-cord for these 4 knots. With the next 2 left cords, tie 2 Reversed Double Half Hitches. The outside cord of this pair of cords becomes the knotting-cord for these 2 knots. Repeat this step on the right.

Step 36. The 2 center cords become the *left* and *right core-cords*. The other 5 cords on the left become the *left knotting-cords*. The other 5 cords on the right become the *right knotting-cords*.

Step 37. Carry the right core-cord diagonally across the right knotting-cords. Tie the right knotting-cords around the right core-cord with Diagonal Double Half Hitches.

Step 38. Carry the left core-cord diagonally across the left knotting-cords. Tie the left knotting-cords around the left core-cord with Diagonal Double Half Hitches.

Step 39. With the 10 center cords, tie 1 Multiple-Strand Square Knot. The 6 center cords become the core-cords and the 2 cords on either side of the core-cords become the knotting-cords.

Step 40. Repeat Steps 32, 33 and 34.

Step 41. With the 4 center cords, tie 3 Square Knots.

Step 42. With the 2 left cords, tie 8 Single Chain Knots. With the next 2 left cords, tie 6 Single Chain Knots. Repeat this step on the right.

Step 43. Repeat the above steps in the following sequence: 36, 37, 38, 32, 33, 34.

Step 44. With the 4 center cords, tie 2 Square Knots. Divide the cords into pairs. Tie 9 Half Hitches on each pair of cords. Tie 1 Double-Strand Overhand Knot below each of the last Half Hitches. Trim all ends to 5″ and untwist cords to form tassels.

Step 45. Attach 6 small screw hooks to the bottom of the molding and hang the knotted sections on the hooks. Attach 2 small screw hooks to the top of the molding for attaching the hanging on the wall. Glue shells to the face of the molding to cover the hooks. Insert shells through various cords at random or in a pattern. Glue them in place.

WOOL WALL HANGING

(6″ by 22″. See Figs. 158, 159 and Plate 58)

MATERIALS

246′ knitting wool; small cardboard tube 6″ long.

METHOD

Step 1. Cut 20 knotting-cords, each 12′ long. Fold all the knotting-cords in half and mount them on the cardboard tube with Clove Hitches. Cut 1 core-cord 2′ long. Lay the center of the core-cord across all the knotting-cords. Tie the knotting-cords around the core-cord with Horizontal Double Half Hitches.

Plate 58. Wool Wall Hanging. Knitting yarn, while difficult to handle, produces a delicate tracery of design. Courtesy Terry Schwartz.

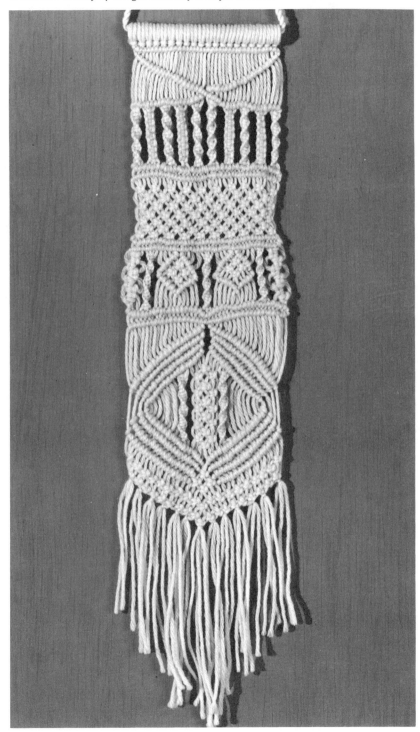

Step 2. Divide the number of cords in half. The left end of the core-cord becomes the *left core-cord*. The other 10 cords on the left become the *left knotting-cords*. The right end of the core-cord becomes the *right core-cord*. The other 10 cords on the right become the *right knotting-cords*.

Step 3. Carry the right core-cord diagonally across the right knotting-cords. Tie the right knotting-cords around the right core-cord with Diagonal Double Half Hitches.

Step 4. Carry the left core-cord diagonally across the left knotting-cords. Tie the left knotting-cords around the left core-cord with Diagonal Double Half Hitches.

Step 5. Cross the left core-cord over the right core-cord and carry it horizontally over the right knotting-cords. Tie the right knotting-cords around the left core-cord with Horizontal Double Half Hitches.

Step 6. Take the right core-cord, which lies under the left core-cord, and carry it horizontally over the left knotting-cords. Tie the left knotting-cords around the right core-cord with Horizontal Double Half Hitches.

Step 7. Carry the ends of the left and right core-cords to the reverse side and thread them through the back of several knots. Trim the ends close to the back of the piece and glue them in place.

Step 8. Divide the cords into groups of 4. Working from the left, tie 16 Half Knots on the 1st, 3rd and 5th groups of 4 cords. Working from the left, tie 8 Square Knots on the 2nd and 4th groups of 4 cords. Repeat this step on the right.

Step 9. The outside left cord becomes the *core-cord*. The other cords become the *knotting-cords*. Carry the core-cord horizontally across all the knotting-cords. Tie the knotting-cords around the core-cord with Horizontal Double Half Hitches.

Step 10. The outside right cord becomes the *core-cord*. The other cords become the *knotting-cords*. Carry the core-cords horizontally across all the knotting-cords. Tie the knotting-cords around the core-cord with Horizontal Double Half Hitches.

Step 11. Beginning with the outside 4 cords on either side, tie 1 row of Square Knots. Tie 6 rows of Alternating Square Knots.

Step 12. Repeat Steps 9 and 10.

Step 13. With the 4 left cords, tie 6 Reversed Double Half Hitches. With the next 4 cords, tie 16 Half Hitches. Repeat this step on the right. With the 4 center cords, tie 16 Half Hitches.

209

Fig. 158

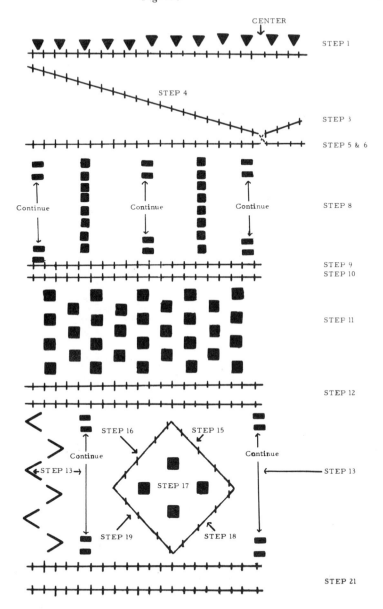

Steps 14 through 19 are worked on the 10 unknotted cords on the left, and will form a diamond pattern of Diagonal Double Half Hitches with 4 Square Knots in the center.

Step 14. The 2 center cords become the *left* and *right core-cords.* The other 4 cords on the left become the *left knotting-cords.* The other 4 cords on the right become the *right knotting-cords.*

Step 15. Carry the right core-cord diagonally across the right knotting-cords. Tie the right knotting-cords around the right core-cord with Diagonal Double Half Hitches.

Step 16. Carry the left core-cord diagonally across the left knotting-cords. Tie the left knotting-cords around the left core-cord with Diagonal Double Half Hitches.

Step 17. With the 4 center cords, tie 1 Square Knot. With the 8 center cords tie 2 Alternating Square Knots. With the 4 center cords, tie 1 Alternating Square Knot.

Step 18. Carry the right core-cord diagonally back to the center across the right knotting-cords. Tie the right knotting-cords around the right core-cord with Diagonal Double Half Hitches.

Step 19. Carry the left core-cord diagonally back to the center across the left knotting-cords. Tie the left knotting-cords around the left core-cord with Diagonal Double Half Hitches.

Step 20. Repeat Steps 14 through 19 with the 10 unknotted cords on the right.

Step 21. Repeat Steps 9 and 10.

Step 22. The 2 center cords become the *left* and *right core-cords.* The 19 cords on the left become the *left knotting-cords.* The other 19 cords on the right become the *right knotting-cords.*

Step 23. Carry the right core-cord diagonally across the right knotting-cords. Tie the right knotting-cords around the right core-cord with Diagonal Double Half Hitches.

Step 24. Carry the left core-cord diagonally across the left knotting-cords. Tie the left knotting-cords around the left core-cord with Diagonal Double Half Hitches.

Step 25. Repeat Steps 22, 23 and 24, three times. On the 2nd row of knots the core-cords will cover only 18 knotting-cords. On the 3rd row of knots the core-cords will cover only 17 knotting-cords. On the 4th row of knots the core-cords will cover only 16 knotting-cords.

Step 26. With the 4 center cords, tie 1 Square Knot. Tie 10 rows of Alternating Square Knots.

Fig. 159

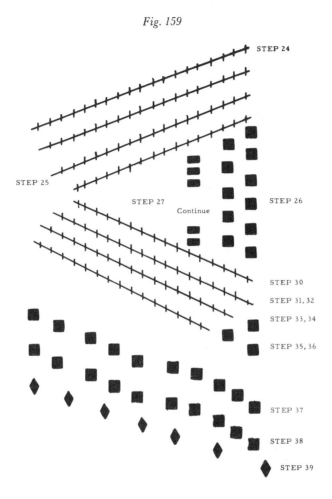

STEP 24

STEP 25

STEP 27

STEP 26

Continue

STEP 30

STEP 31, 32

STEP 33, 34

STEP 35, 36

STEP 37

STEP 38

STEP 39

Step 27. With the 13th, 14th, 15th and 16th cords from the left, tie 12 Half Knots. Repeat this step on the right.

Step 28. Divide the number of cords in half. The 4th cord from the left becomes the *left core-cord*. The 4th cord from the right becomes the *right core-cord*. The other cords between the core-cords become the *left* and *right knotting-cords*.

Step 29. Carry the right core-cord diagonally back to the center across the right knotting-cords. Tie the right knotting-cords around the right core-cord with Diagonal Double Half Hitches.

Step 30. Carry the left core-cord diagonally back to the center across the left knotting-cords. Tie the left knotting-cords around the left core-cord with Diagonal Double Half Hitches.

Step 31. Divide the number of cords in half. The 3rd cord from the left becomes the *left core-cord*. The 3rd cord from the right becomes the *right core-cord*.

Step 32. Repeat Steps 29 and 30.

Step 33. Divide the number of cords in half. The 2nd cord from the left becomes the *left core-cord*. The outside right cord becomes the *right core-core-cord*.

Step 34. Repeat Steps 29 and 30, tying only 16 Diagonal Double Half Hitches. With the 4 center cords, tie 1 Square Knot.

Step 35. Divide the number of cords in half. The outside left cord becomes the *left core-cord*. The outside right cord becomes the *right core-cord*.

Step 36. Repeat Steps 29 and 30, tying only 15 Diagonal Double Half Hitches. With the 8 center cords, tie 2 Alternating Square Knots. With the 4 center cords, tie 1 Alternating Square Knot.

Step 37. Beginning with the outside 4 cords on either side, tie 1 diagonal row of Alternating Square Knots, 1″ below the last row of knots.

Step 38. Beginning with the outside 4 cords on either side, tie 1 diagonal row of Alternating Square Knots, 1/2″ below the last row of knots.

Step 39. With the 4 center cords, tie 1 Multiple-Strand Overhand Knot. Divide the balance of the cords into groups of 3. Tie 1 Multiple-Strand Overhand Knot on each group of 3 cords. Trim all ends to 6″.

Step 40. Cut 2 cords, each 2′ long. Twist the 2 cords together. Insert the ends of both cords through the cardboard tube. Tie the 2 ends of the cords together with 1 Multiple-Strand Overhand Knot. Slide the knot inside the tube.

JUTE WALL HANGING

(6" by 38". See Figs. 160-162, Plate 59 and Color Plate VI)

MATERIALS

336′ Lily Jute-Tone; 1 cardboard tube 6″ long.

METHOD

Step 1. Cut 18 knotting-cords, each 24′ long. Fold all the knotting-cords in half and mount them on the cardboard tube with Clove Hitches.

Step 2. The outside left cord becomes the *left core-cord*. The outside right cord becomes the *right core-cord*. The balance of the cords become the knotting-cords.

Step 3. Carry the left core-cord horizontally across the knotting-cords and the right core-cord. Tie the knotting-cords and the right core-cord around the left core-cord with Horizontal Double Half Hitches. Fold the end of the left core-cord down beside the knotting-cords.

Step 4. Carry the right core-cord horizontally across the knotting-cords. Tie the knotting-cords around the right core-cord with Horizontal Double Half Hitches. The left core-cord will not be tied around the right core-cord.

Step 5. With the 4 left cords, tie 12 Half Knots. With the next 4 cords, tie 6 Square Knots. Repeat this step on the right.

Steps 6 through 11 will form a diamond pattern of Diagonal Double Half Hitches with 4 Square Knots in the center.

Step 6. The 2 center cords become the *left* and *right core-cords*. The 9 unknotted cords on the left become the *left knotting-cords*. The 9 unknotted cords on the right become the *right knotting-cords*.

Step 7. Carry the right core-cord diagonally across the right knotting-cords. Tie the right knotting-cords around the right core-cord with Diagonal Double Half Hitches.

Step 8. Carry the left core-cord diagonally across the left knotting-cords. Tie the left knotting-cords around the left core-cord with Diagonal Double Half Hitches.

Step 9. With the 4 center cords, tie 1 Square Knot. With the 8 center cords, tie 2 Alternating Square Knots. With the 4 center cords, tie 1 Square Knot.

Fig. 160

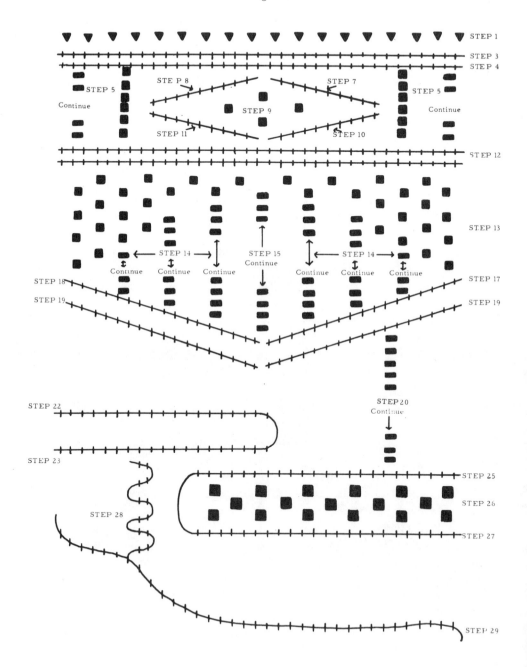

Step 10. Carry the right core-cord diagonally back to the center across the right knotting-cords. Tie the right knotting-cords around the right core-cord with Diagonal Double Half Hitches.

Step 11. Carry the left core-cord diagonally back to the center across the left knotting-cords. Tie the left knotting-cords around the left core-cord with Diagonal Double Half Hitches.

Step 12. Repeat Steps 2, 3 and 4.

Step 13. Leaving the 2 outside cords on each side free, tie 1 row of Square Knots. Beginning with the 4 left cords, tie 4 Alternating Square Knots. Leaving the 2 outside left cords free, tie 2 Alternating Square Knots. Beginning with the 4 left cords, tie 2 Alternating Square Knots. Leaving the 2 outside left cords free, tie 2 Alternating Square Knots. Beginning with the 4 left cords, tie 2 Alternating Square Knots. Leaving the 2 outside left cords free, tie 1 Alternating Square Knot. With the 4 left cords, tie 1 Alternating Square Knot. Repeat this step on the right.

Step 14. With the 5th, 6th, 7th and 8th cords from the left, tie 6 Half Knots. With the 9th, 10th, 11th and 12th cords from the left, tie 15 Half Knots. With the 13th, 14th, 15th and 16th cords from the left, tie 21 Half Knots. Repeat this step on the right.

Step 15. With the 4 center cords, tie 24 Half Knots.

Step 16. Divide the number of cords in half. The outside left cord becomes the *left core-cord*. The other 17 cords on the left become the *left knotting-cords*. The outside right cord becomes the *right core-cord*. The other 17 cords on the right become the *right knotting-cords*.

Step 17. Carry the right core-cord diagonally across the right knotting-cords. Tie the right knotting-cords around the right core-cord with Diagonal Double Half Hitches.

Step 18. Carry the left core-cord diagonally across the left knotting-cords. Tie the left knotting-cords around the left core-cord with Diagonal Double Half Hitches.

Step 19. Repeat Steps 16, 17 and 18.

Step 20. With the 8th, 9th, 10th and 11th cords from the right, tie 21 Half Knots.

Step 21. The outside left cord becomes the *left core-cord*. The next 19 cords on the left become the *left knotting-cords*.

Step 22. At a point 1½" below the beginning of the Diagonal Double Half Hitches tied in Step 19, carry the left core-cord horizontally across the left knotting-cords. Tie the left knotting-cords around the left core-cord with Horizontal Double Half Hitches.

Step 23. Carry the left core-cord horizontally back to the left side across the left knotting-cords, ½″ below the last row of knots. Tie the left knotting-cords around the left core-cord with Horizontal Double Half Hitches.

Step 24. The outside right cord becomes the right core-cord. The next 23 cords on the right become the *right knotting-cords*.

Step 25. At a point directly below the last Half Knot tied in Step 20, carry the right core-cord horizontally across the right knotting-cords. Tie the right knotting-cords around the right core-cord with Horizontal Double Half Hitches.

Step 26. Beginning with the 4 right cords, tie 1 row of 6 Square Knots. Leaving the 2 outside right cords free, tie 5 Alternating Square Knots. Beginning with the 4 right cords, tie 6 Alternating Square Knots.

Step 27. Carry the right core-cord horizontally back to the right side across the left knotting-cords, directly below the last row of Alternating Square Knots. Tie the right knotting-cords around the right core-cord with Horizontal Double Half Hitches.

Step 28. The 8th cord from the left becomes the *left core-cord*. The next 2 cords from the left become the *left knotting-cords*. Carry the left core-cord back and forth across the left knotting-cords 6 times, tying the knotting-cords around the core-cord with Horizontal Double Half Hitches. *(See Fig. 160.)*

Step 29. The outside left cord becomes the *left core-cord*. The balance of the cords become the *knotting-cords*. Carry the left core-cord in an irregular line across all the knotting-cords. *(See Fig. 160.)* Tie all the knotting-cords around the left core-cord with Diagonal and Horizontal Double Half Hitches.

Step 30. Carry the left core-cord horizontally back to the left side across all the knotting-cords. Tie the knotting-cords around the left core-cord with Horizontal Double Half Hitches.

Steps 31 through 36 will form an "X" pattern of Alternating Square Knots with Reversed Double Half Hitches on the outside of the edges.

Step 31. Beginning with the 4 left cords, tie 1 diagonal row of 8 Alternating Square Knots.

Step 32. Beginning with the 4 right cords, tie 1 diagonal row of 8 Alternating Square Knots.

Step 33. With the 4 center cords, tie 1 Alternating Square Knot.

Step 34. Divide the 15 cords on the left into groups of 3. The outside cord of each group will be the knotting-cord. The 2 inside cords of each

Fig. 161

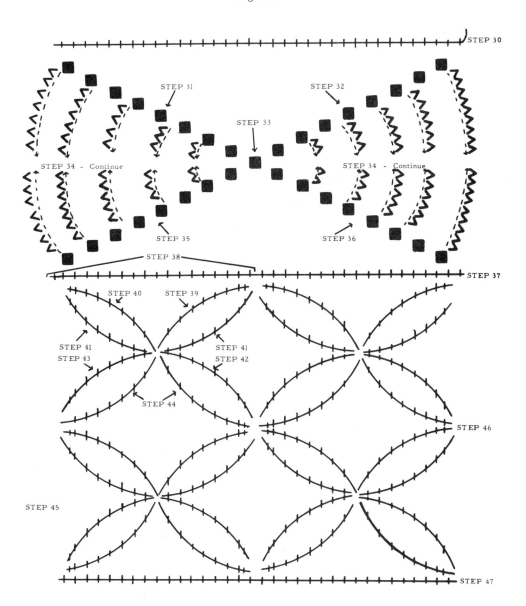

group will be the core-cords. Working from the outside, tie the following number of Reversed Double Half Hitches on each group of 3 cords: 20, 15, 9, 6, 3.

Step 35. Beginning with the 4 cords directly to the left of center, tie 1 diagonal row of 8 Alternating Square Knots.

Step 36. Beginning with the 4 cords directly to the right of center, tie 1 diagonal row of 8 Alternating Square Knots.

Step 37. The outside left cord becomes the *left core-cord*. The balance of the cords become the *knotting-cords*. Carry the left core-cord horizontally across the knotting-cords. Tie the knotting-cords around the left core-cord with Horizontal Double Half Hitches.

Steps 38 through 45 are worked on the 18 left cords.

Step 38. Divide the number of cords in half. The outside left core becomes the *left core-cord*. The other 8 cords on the left become the *left knotting-cords*. The outside right cord becomes the *right core-cord*. The other 8 cords on the right become the *right knotting-cords*.

Step 39. Carry the right core-cord diagonally across the right knotting-cords. Curve the core-cord upward slightly in the center. Tie the right knotting-cords around the right core-cord with Diagonal Double Half Hitches.

Step 40. Carry the left core-cord diagonally across the left knotting-cords. Curve the core-cord upward slightly in the center. Tie the left knotting-cords around the right core-cord with Diagonal Double Half Hitches.

Step 41. Repeat Steps 38, 39 and 40, curving the core-cord slightly downward in the center, instead of upward.

Step 42. Cross the left core-cord over the right core-cord and carry it diagonally over the right knotting-cords. Curve the core-cord upward slightly in the center. Tie the right knotting-cords around the left core-cord with Diagonal Double Half Hitches.

Step 43. Take the right core-cord, which lies under the left core-cord, and carry it diagonally *over* the left knotting-cords. Curve the core-cord upward slightly in the center. Tie the left knotting-cords around the right core-cord with Diagonal Double Half Hitches.

Step 44. Repeat Steps 42 and 43, curving the core-cord downward slightly in the center, instead of upward.

Step 45. Repeat Steps 38 through 44.

Step 46. Repeat Steps 38 through 45 on the 18 right cords.

Step 47. Repeat Step 37.

Step 48. With the 5th, 6th, 7th and 8th cords from the left, tie 14 Half Knots. Repeat this step on the right.

Step 49. Divide the 12 center cords into groups of 4. Tie 2 Square Knots on each group of 4 cords.

Step 50. Divide the 8 center cords into groups of 4. Tie 1 Alternating Square Knot on each group of 4 cords. Tie 1 Square Knot on each group of 4 cords.

Step 51. Repeat Steps 49 and 50.

Step 52. With the 4 center cords, tie 1 Alternating Square Knot. With the 4 center cords, tie 1 Square Knot.

Steps 53, 54 and 55 are worked on the 12 center cords.

Step 53. Divide the number of cords in half. The outside left cord becomes the *left core-cord*. The other 5 cords on the left become the *left knotting-cords*. The outside right cord becomes the *right core-cord*. The other 5 cords on the right become the *right knotting-cords*.

Step 54. Carry the right core-cord diagonally across the right knotting-cords. Tie the right knotting-cords around the right core-cord with Diagonal Double Half Hitches.

Step 55. Carry the left core-cord diagonally across the left knotting-cords. Tie the left knotting-cords around the left core-cord with Diagonal Double Half Hitches.

Step 56. Repeat Steps 53, 54 and 55 on the 16 center cords.

Step 57. Repeat Steps 53, 54 and 55 on the 20 center cords.

Step 58. Repeat Steps 53, 54 and 55 on the 22 center cords.

Step 59. With the 4 center cords, tie 1 Square Knot.

Step 60. Beginning with the 7th, 8th, 9th and 10th cords from the left, tie 1 diagonal row of 5 Alternating Square Knots.

Step 61. The 4th cord from the left becomes the *left core-cord*. The next 12 cords from the left become the *left knotting-cords*. Tie the left knotting-cords around the left core-cord with Diagonal Double Half Hitches. Repeat this step on the right.

Step 62. The 3rd cord from the left becomes the *left core-cord*. The next 12 cords from the left become the *left knotting-cords*. Tie the left knotting cords around the left core-cord with Diagonal Double Half Hitches. Repeat this step on the right.

Step 63. The 2nd cord from the left becomes the *left core-cord*. The next 11 cords from the left become the *left knotting-cords*. Tie the left knotting-cords around the left core-cord with Diagonal Double Half Hitches. Repeat this step on the right.

Fig. 162

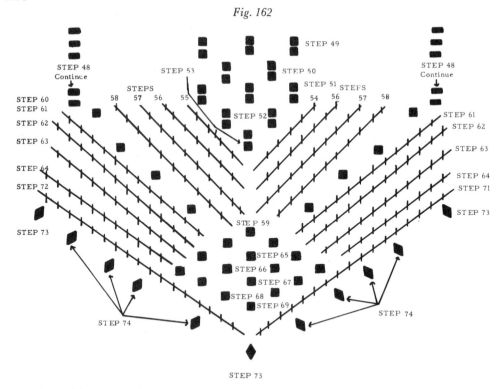

STEP 49

STEP 48
Continue

STEP 53

STEP 50

STEP 48
Continue

STEPS
58   57   56   55

STEP 51   STEPS
54   56   57   58

STEP 60
STEP 61

STEP 62

STEP 63

STEP 64

STEP 72

STEP 52

STEP 61

STEP 62

STEP 63

STEP 64

STEP 71

STEP 73

STEP 73

STEP 59

STEP 65
STEP 66
STEP 67
STEP 68
STEP 69

STEP 74

STEP 74

STEP 74

STEP 73

Step 64. The outside left cord becomes the *left core-cord*. The next 11 cords from the left become the *left knotting-cords*. Tie the left knotting-cords around the left core-cord with Diagonal Double Half Hitches. Repeat this step on the right.

Step 65. Divide the 12 center cords into groups of 4. Tie 1 Alternating Square Knot on each group of 4 cords.

Step 66. Divide the 16 center cords into groups of 4. Tie 1 Alternating Square Knot on each group of 4 cords.

Step 67. Repeat Step 65.

Step 68. Divide the 8 center cords into groups of 4. Tie 1 Alternating Square Knot on each group of 4 cords.

Step 69. With the 4 center cords, tie 1 Alternating Square Knot.

Step 70. Divide the number of cords in half. The outside left cord becomes the *left core-cord*. The other 17 cords on the left become the *left knotting-cords*. The outside right cord becomes the *right core-cord*. The other 17 cords on the right become the *right knotting-cords*.

Step 71. Carry the right core-cord diagonally across the right knotting-cords. Tie the right knotting-cords around the right core-cord with Diagonal Double Half Hitches.

Step 72. Carry the left core-cord diagonally across the left knotting-cords. Tie the left knotting-cords around the left core-cord with Diagonal Double Half Hitches.

Step 73. With the 4 left cords, tie 1 Multiple-Strand Overhand Knot. With the 4 right cords, tie 1 Multiple-Strand Overhand Knot. With the 4 center cords, tie 1 Multiple-Strand Overhand Knot.

Step 74. Divide the balance of the cords into groups of 3. Tie 1 Multiple-Strand Overhand Knot on each group of 3 cords. Trim all ends to 8″.

Step 75. Cut 2 cords, each 2′ long. Twist the 2 cords together. Insert the ends of both cords through the cardboard tube. Tie the ends of the cords together with 1 Multiple-Strand Overhand Knot. Slide the knot inside the tube.

Plate 59. Jute Wall Hanging. Note the use of several free form knotting patterns in the center for accent. It would be particularly useful in those odd, skinny wall areas where conventional wall decorations fail. Courtesy Terry Schwartz.

SISAL WALL HANGING

(18" by 40". See Figs. 163, 164; Plate 60 and Color Plate VIII)

MATERIALS

202' of ¼" brown sisal; 202' of ¼" yellow sisal; 200' of ¼" natural sisal; ¼" wooden dowel, 22" long; 12 small beads.

METHOD

Step 1. Cut 8 brown, 8 yellow and 8 natural cords, each 25' long. Fold all the cords in half and mount on the dowel with Clove Hitches in the following sequence: 4 brown, 2 yellow, 2 natural, 2 yellow, 4 natural, 2 yellow, 2 natural, 2 yellow, 4 brown.

Step 2. Beginning with the outside 4 cords on either side, tie 1 row of Square Knots. Tie 2 rows of Alternating Square Knots.

Step 3. The 8th cord from the right becomes the *1st core-cord*. The 7 cords directly to its right become the *1st group of knotting-cords*. Carry the 1st core-cord diagonally across the 1st group of knotting-cords. Tie the 1st group of knotting-cords around the 1st core-cord with Diagonal Double Half Hitches.

Step 4. The 16th cord from the right becomes the *2nd core-cord*. The 15 cords directly to its right become the *2nd group of knotting-cords*. Carry the 2nd core-cord diagonally across the 2nd group of knotting-cords. Tie the 2nd group of knotting-cords around the 2nd core-cord with Diagonal Double Half Hitches.

Step 5. The 24th cord from the right becomes the *3rd core-cord*. The 14 cords directly to its right become the *3rd group of knotting-cords*. Carry the 3rd core-cord diagonally across the 3rd group of knotting-cords. Tie the 3rd group of knotting-cords around the 3rd core-cord with Diagonal Double Half Hitches.

Step 6. The 32nd cord from the right becomes the *4th core-cord*. The 14 cords directly to its *right become the 4th group of knotting-cords*. Carry the 4th core-cord diagonally across the 4th group of knotting-cords. Tie the 4th group of knotting-cords around the 4th core-cord with Diagonal Double Half Hitches.

Step 7. The 40th cord from the right becomes the *5th core-cord*. The 14 cords directly to its right become the *5th group of knotting-cords*. Carry the 5th core-cord diagonally across the 5th group of knotting-cords. Tie the 5th group of knotting-cords around the 5th core-cord with Diagonal Double Half Hitches.

Step 8. The outside left-cord becomes the *6th core-cord*. The 14 cords directly to its right become the *6th group of knotting-cords*. Carry the 6th core-cord diagonally across the 6th group of knotting-cords. Tie the 6th group of knotting-cords around the 6th core-cord with Diagonal Double Half Hitches.

Step 9. The outside left cord becomes the *7th core-cord*. The 6 cords directly to its right become the *7th group of knotting-cords*. Carry the 7th core-cord diagonally across the 7th group of knotting-cords, 1″ below the knots tied in Step 8.

Step 10. Carry the 6th core-cord back to the left across the 6th group of knotting-cords. Tie the 6th group of knotting-cords around the 6th core-cord with Diagonal Double Half Hitches.

Step 11. Carry the 5th core-cord back to the left across the 5th group of knotting-cords. Tie the 5th group of knotting-cords around the 5th core-cord with Diagonal Double Half Hitches.

Step 12. Carry the 4th core-cord back to the left across the 4th group of knotting-cords. Tie the 4th group of knotting-cords around the 4th core-cord with Diagonal Double Half Hitches.

Step 13. Carry the 3rd core-cord back to the left across the 3rd group of knotting-cords. Tie the 3rd group of knotting-cords around the 3rd core-cord with Diagonal Double Half Hitches.

Step 14. Carry the 2nd core-cord back to the left across the 2nd group of knotting-cords. Tie the 2nd group of knotting-cords around the 2nd core-cord with Diagonal Double Half Hitches.

Step 15. Divide the cords into groups of 4. Tie 12 Square Knots on each group of 4 cords.

Step 16. Number the groups of Square Knots, from the left. Cross the 3rd group of Square Knots over the 4th group of Square Knots. Cross the 5th group of Square Knots over the 3rd and 4th group of Square Knots.

Step 17. Cross the 6th group of Square Knots over the 7th group of Square Knots.

Step 18. Cross the 10th group of Square Knots over the 9th group of Square Knots. Cross the 8th group of Square Knots over the 9th and 10th group of Square Knots.

Step 19. Leaving the 2 outside cords on each side free, and the 4 center cords free, tie 1 row of Square Knots.

224

Fig. 163

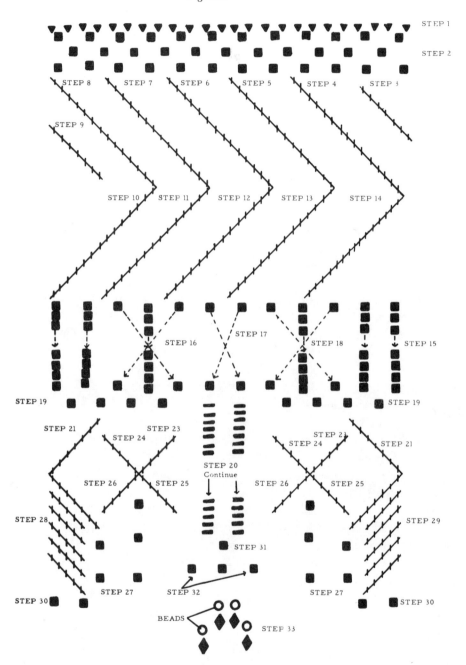

STEP 1

STEP 2

STEP 8   STEP 7   STEP 6   STEP 5   STEP 4   STEP 3

STEP 9

STEP 10   STEP 11   STEP 12   STEP 13   STEP 14

STEP 16   STEP 17   STEP 18   STEP 15

STEP 19   STEP 19

STEP 21   STEP 23   STEP 23   STEP 21
STEP 24   STEP 24
STEP 20
Continue
STEP 26   STEP 25   STEP 26   STEP 25

STEP 28   STEP 29

STEP 31

STEP 30   STEP 27   STEP 32   STEP 27   STEP 30

BEADS   STEP 33

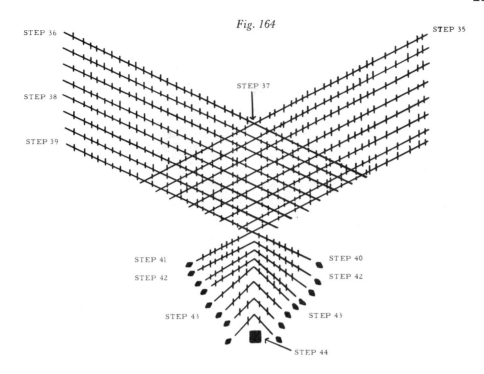

STEP 36   STEP 35
STEP 37
STEP 38
STEP 39
STEP 41   STEP 40
STEP 42   STEP 42
STEP 43   STEP 43
STEP 44

Fig. 164

Step 20. With the 4 cords directly to the left of center, tie 17 Half Knots. With the 4 cords directly to the right of center, tie 17 Half Knots.

Step 21. The 8th cord from the left becomes the *core-cord*. The 7 cords directly to its left become the *knotting-cords*. Carry the core-cord diagonally across the knotting-cords. Tie the knotting-cords around the core-cord with Diagonal Double Half Hitches. Carry the core-cord diagonally back toward the center across the knotting-cords. Tie the knotting-cords around the core-cord with Diagonal Double Half Hitches. Repeat this step on the right. *Steps 22 through 26 will form an "X" pattern of Diagonal Double Half Hitches and is worked on the unknotted yellow and white cords between the knots tied in Steps 20 and 21.*

Step 22. Divide the number of cords by half. The outside left cord becomes the *left core-cord*. The other 5 cords on the left become the *left knotting-cords*. The outside right cord becomes the *right core-cord*. The other 5 cords on the right become the *right knotting-cords*.

Step 23. Carry the right core-cord diagonally across the right knotting-cords. Tie the right knotting-cords around the right core-cord with Diagonal Double Half Hitches.

Step 24. Carry the left core-cord diagonally across the left knotting-cords. Tie the left knotting-cords around the left core-cord with Diagonal Double Half Hitches.

Step 25. Cross the left core-cord over the right core-cord and carry it diagonally over the right knotting-cords. Tie the right knotting-cords around the left core-cord with Diagonal Double Half Hitches.

Step 26. Take the right core-cord, which lies under the left core-cord, and carry it diagonally *over* the left knotting-cords. Tie the left knotting-cords around the right core-cord with Diagonal Double Half Hitches.

Step 27. With the 6th, 7th, 8th and 9th cords from the left, tie 2 Square Knots. With the 12th and 17th cords from the left, tie 1 Square Knot over the 14th and 15th cords from the left. With the 11th and 18th cords from the left, tie 1 Square Knot over the 14th and 15th cords from the left. With the 13th and 16th cords from the left, tie 1 Square Knot over the 14th and 15th cords from the left. Repeat this step on the right.

Step 28. The outside left cord becomes the core-cord. The 5 cords directly to its right become the knotting-cords. Carry the core-cord diagonally across the knotting-cords. Tie the knotting-cords around the core-cord with Diagonal Double Half Hitches. Repeat this step 4 more times.

Step 29. Repeat Step 28 on the right.

Step 30. With the 4 left cords, tie 1 Square Knot. With the next 4 cords, tie 1 Square Knot. Repeat this step on the right.

Step 31. With the 4 center cords, tie 2 Square Knots.

Step 32. With the 19th, 20th, 21st and 22nd cords from the left, tie 1 Square Knot. Repeat this step on the right.

Step 33. String 1 bead on each of the 4 center cords. Tie 1 Simple Overhand Knot below the 2 center beads, 2" below the last Square Knot. Tie 1 Simple Overhand Knot below the 2 other beads, 3" below the last Square Knot.

Step 34. Divide the number of cords by half. The outside left cord becomes the *left core-cord*. The other 23 cords on the left become the *left knotting-cords*. The outside right cord becomes the *right core-cord*. The other 23 cords on the right become the *right knotting-cords*.

Step 35. Carry the right core-cord diagonally across the right knotting-cords. Tie the right knotting-cords around the right core-cord with Diagonal Double Half Hitches.

Step 36. Carry the left core-cord diagonally across the left knotting-cords. Tie the left knotting-cords around the left core-cord with Diagonal Double Half Hitches.

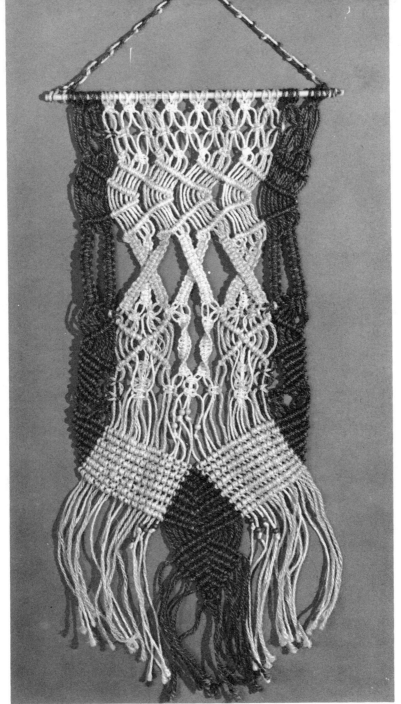

Plate 60. Sisal Wall Hanging. This large wall hanging gains much of its appeal through its effective use of open and solid areas and the colors of the hand-dyed sisal. Courtesy Irene Michaud.

Step 37. Cross the left core-cord over the right core-cord. Tie the right core-cord around the left core-cord with 1 Diagonal Double Half Hitch.

Step 38. Repeat Steps 34 through 37, six times.

Step 39. Repeat Steps 34 through 36, one time.

Step 40. Cross the left core-cord over the right core-cord and carry it diagonally over 7 right knotting-cords. Tie the 7 right knotting-cords around the left core-cord with Diagonal Double Half Hitches. Tie the core-cord and last knotting-cord together with 1 Double-Strand Overhand Knot.

Step 41. Take the right core-cord, which lies under the left core-cord, and carry it diagonally *over* 7 left knotting-cords. Tie the 7 left knotting-cords around the right core-cord with Diagonal Double Half Hitches. Tie the core-cord and last knotting-cord together with 1 Double-Strand Overhand Knot.

Step 42. Repeat Steps 40 and 41, one time.

Step 43. Repeat Steps 40 and 41, six times, decreasing the number of knotting cords by 1 with each step.

Step 44. With the 4 center cords, tie 1 Square Knot.

Step 45. String 1 bead on the 13th, 14th, 15th and 16th cords from the left. Tie 1 Simple Overhand Knot below each bead, from 1″ to 3″ below the last row of Diagonal Double Half Hitches. Trim all ends to 8 to 12 inches long.

Step 46. Cut 1 brown and 1 yellow cord, each 2½′ long. Tie the 2 cords together with Single Chain Knots. Tie the ends of the sinnet to each end of the dowel with 1 Double-Strand Overhand Knot.

SCARECROW WALL HANGING

(3' by 3½'. See Figs. 165-168, Plate 61 and Color Plate IV)

MATERIALS

75' white rug yarn; 122' dark blue rug yarn; 20' light blue rug yarn; 57' dark green rug yarn; one 6" embroidery hoop; 1 pair 7" embroidery hoops; 2 pair 4½" by 9" oval embroidery hoops; 1 drapery pole, 3' long; 1 pair wooden finials; 40 round yellow beads; 7 round red beads; 20 square blue beads; 5 rings, 1" in diameter; backing felt 36" by 50".

Plate 61. Scarecrow Wall Hanging. Embroidery hoops define the body shapes of this scarecrow. Each section was knotted separately, then assembled and stitched on the felt.

230

Fig. 165

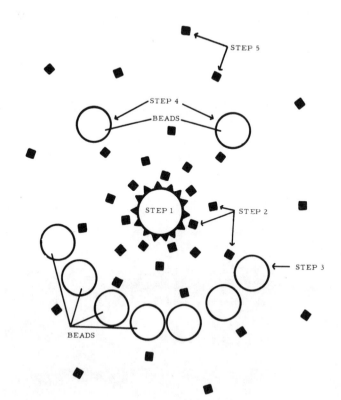

METHOD

FACE (*See Fig. 165*)

Step 1. Cut 14 white cords, each 4′ long. Fold all the cords in half and mount them on one of the 1″ rings with Clove Hitches. Pin the ring in the center of the 6″ embroidery hoop.

Step 2. Divide the cords into groups of 4. Tie 1 Square Knot on each group of 4 cords. Tie 2 rows of Alternating Square Knots.

Step 3. Divide 14 cords into pairs. String 1 red bead on each pair of cords. This will become the mouth.

Step 4. Leave 2 cords free on each side of the mouth. String 1 yellow bead on the next 2 cords on each side. These become the eyes.

Step 5. Tie 2 rows of Alternating Square Knots.

Step 6. Wrap the ends of each cord around the embroidery hoop. Glue to the outside of the hoop. Cut strands of rug yarn, approximately 4″ to 8″ long. Tie these to the top of the hoop for hair. Wrap short strands of white yarn around the exposed portion of the embroidery hoop. Sew 1 yellow bead in the center ring for a nose.

BODY TOP (*See Fig. 166*)

Step 7. Cut 1 dark blue cord 12″ long. String 7 beads on the cord. Tie the cords across the center of one of the 7″ embroidery hoops. Cut 8 dark blue and 8 dark green cords, each 4′ long. Tie the center of these cords around the center cord with Simple Overhand Knots in the following sequence:
2 dark green, 1 bead, 2 dark green, 1 bead, 2 dark blue, 1 bead, 2 dark blue, 1 bead, 2 dark blue, 1 bead, 2 dark blue, 1 bead, 2 dark green, 1 bead, 2 dark green.

Step 8. On one side of the beads, divide the cords into groups of 4. Tie 1 Square Knot on each group of 4 cords.

Step 9. Tie 2 rows of Alternating Square Knots.

Step 10. Tie 2 rows of Alternating Square Knots, decreasing each row by 1 Square Knot.

Step 11. Repeat Steps 8, 9 and 10 on the other side of the beads.

Step 12. Wrap the ends of each cord around the embroidery hoop. Glue to the outside of the hoop. Wrap short strands of dark green yarn around the exposed portion of the embroidery hoop.

BODY BOTTOM

Step 13. Repeat Steps 7 through 12, using all dark green yarn.

ARMS (*See Fig. 167*)

Step 14. Cut 2 light blue and 4 dark blue cords, each, 2′ long. Fold all the cords in half and mount on one of the 1″ rings with Clove Hitches in the following sequence: 1 light blue, 4 dark blue, 1 light blue. Tie the small ring to the inside of one end of 1 of the oval embroidery hoops.

Step 15. Divide the cords into groups of 4. Tie 1 Square Knot on each group of 4 cords. Wrap the 2 outside cords on either side around the embroidery hoop.

232

Step 16. Tie 1 row of Alternating Square Knots. Wrap the 2 outside cords on either side around the embroidery hoop. Repeat this step 12 times.

Step 17. Divide the 10 center cords into pairs. String 1 yellow bead on each pair of cords.

Step 18. Tie 3 Alternating Square Knots.

Step 19. Wrap the ends of each cord around the embroidery hoop. Divide the 10 center cords into pairs. String 1 blue bead on each pair of cords. Tie the 2 outside cords to the embroidery hoop. Tie 1 Double-Strand Overhand Knot outside each of the blue beads. Trim the ends to 1". Wrap short strands of light green yarn around the exposed portion of the embroidery hoop.

Step 20. Repeat Steps 14 through 19 for the 2nd arm.

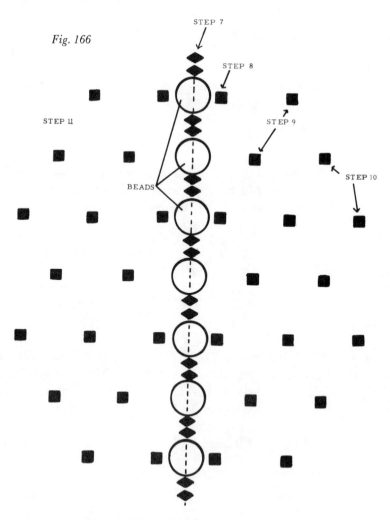

Fig. 166

STEP 7

STEP 8

STEP 11

STEP 9

STEP 10

BEADS

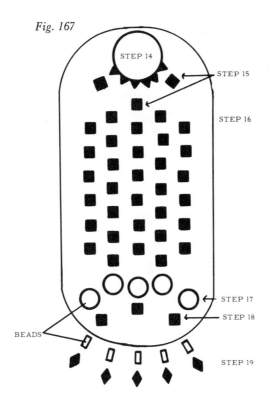

Fig. 167

STEP 14

STEP 15

STEP 16

STEP 17

STEP 18

BEADS

STEP 19

LEGS *(See Fig. 168)*

Step 21. Cut 2 dark green and 6 dark blue cords, each, 4′ long. Fold all the cords in half and mount them on one of the 1″ rings with Clove Hitches in the following sequence: 3 dark blue, 2 green, 3 dark blue. Tie the small ring to the inside of one end of one of the oval embroidery hoops.

Step 22. Divide the number of cords in half. The outside left cord becomes the *left core-cord*. The other 7 cords on the left become the *left knotting-cords*. The outside right cord becomes the *right core-cord*. The other 7 cords on the right become the *right knotting-cords*.

Step 23. Carry the right core-cord under the embroidery hoop and back around diagonally over the right knotting-cords. Tie the right knotting-cords around the right core-cord with Diagonal Double Half Hitches.

Step 24. Carry the left core-cord under the embroidery hoop and back around diagonally over the left knotting-cords. Tie the left knotting-cords around the left core-cord with Diagonal Double Half Hitches.

Step 25. With the 4 center cords, tie 1 Square Knot.

Step 26. Repeat Steps 22 through 25 four times.

234

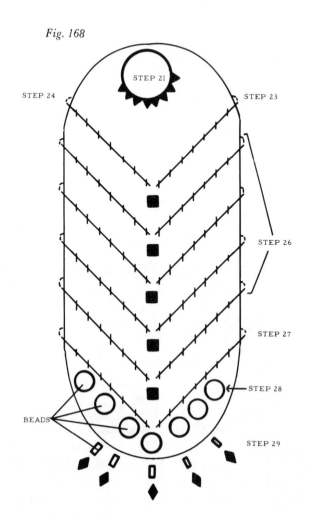

Fig. 168

STEP 21
STEP 24
STEP 23
STEP 26
STEP 27
STEP 28
BEADS
STEP 29

Step 27. Repeat Steps 22 through 24.

Step 28. Leaving the outside cord on each side free, divide the balance of the cords into pairs. String 1 yellow bead on each pair of cords.

Step 29. Wrap the ends of each cord around the embroidery hoop. Tie the 4 outside cords to the embroidery hoop. Divide the balance of the cords into pairs. String 1 blue bead on each pair of cords. Tie 1 Double-Strand Overhand Knot outside each of the blue beads. Trim the ends to 1″. Wrap a short strand of light blue yarn around the exposed portion of the embroidery hoop.

Step 30. Repeat Steps 21 through 29 for the other leg.

Step 31. Fold under 4″ across the top and bottom of the backing felt and sew in place. Arrange the pieces of the body on the center of the backing felt. Sew in place. Place stitches between the knots so that the thread does not show.

Step 32. Cut pieces of light and dark green yarn, 3″ to 9″ long. Glue to the surface of the backing felt across the bottom. Insert drapery pole with finials attached, through the top of the backing felt. Cut 6 dark green cords, each 3½′ long. Twist all the cords together. Tie the ends of the rope to both ends of the drapery pole. Attach 3 dark green tassels to the hanging rope.

CHRISTMAS TREE

(25" by 42". See Figs. 169-172, Plate 62 and Color Plate V)

The following materials and instructions will produce a tree which may be used as a wall hanging (See Plate 62). If you tie 2 or more trees, and fasten them together, you will have a free-standing tree to stand on a table or on the floor (See Color Plate V).

MATERIALS

378' red sisal; 384' green sisal; 10' of ¾" lath.

METHOD

Step 1. Draw *fig. 169* on the knotting board. Keep the sides of the piece pinned to the outside of the figure as the knotting progresses. Use the horizontal lines as guides when knotting. Cut 2 red cords, each 27' long. Fold the cords in half and pin the folds to the knotting board side-by-side. Tie 3 Square Knots.

Step 2. Cut 2 red cords, each 27' long. Fold the cords in half and pin 1 cord on each side of the last Square Knot tied in Step 1. Tie 3 rows of Alternating Square Knots.

Step 3. Cut 2 red cords, each 27' long. Fold the cords in half and pin 1 cord on each side of the last Alternating Square Knots tied in Step 2. Tie 4 rows of Alternating Square Knots.

Step 4. With the 4 left cords, tie 2 Square Knots. Repeat this step on the right.

Step 5. Cut 1 green core-cord, 27' long. Tie 1 Simple Overhand Knot in the center of the cord. Pin the Overhand Knot between the 2 center cords. The left end of the green core-cord becomes the *left core-cord*. The right end of the green core-cord becomes the *right core-cord*. The 6 red cords on the right become the *right core-cords*. The 6 red cords on the left become the *left core-cords*.

Step 6. Carry the right core-cord diagonally across the right knotting-cords. Tie the right knotting-cords around the right core-cord with Diagonal Double Half Hitches.

Step 7. Carry the left core-cord diagonally across the left knotting-cords. Tie the left knotting-cords around the left core-cord with Diagonal Double Half Hitches.

Step 8. Cut 2 green knotting-cords, each 27' long. Fold the cords in half and mount them on the right and left core-cords with Clove Hitches.

Plate 62. Christmas Tree. Save the live trees and decorate with an "I made it myself" tree. The hand-dyed sisal was tied into a loosely knotted tree-shape. Wire was sewn to the inside of the bottom and shaped into an unusual curved three-dimensional wall hanging.

Step 9. Cut 1 green core-cord 27′ long. Tie 1 Simple Overhand Knot in the center of the cord. Pin the Overhand Knot between the 2 center cords 1″ below the Simple Overhand Knot in Step 5. The left end of the green core-cord becomes the *left core-cord*. The right end of the green core-cord becomes the *right core-cord*. The 6 red and 3 green cords on the left become the left knotting-cords. The 6 red and 3 green cords on the right become the right knotting-cords.

Step 10. Carry the right core-cord diagonally across the right knotting-cords, 1″ below the last row of knots. Tie the right knotting-cords around the right core-cord with Diagonal Double Half Hitches.

Fig. 169

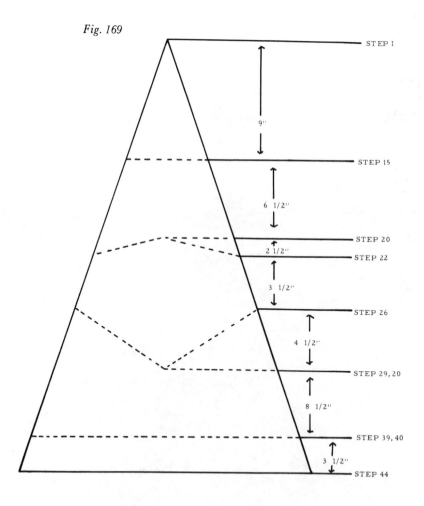

Step 11. Carry the left core-cord diagonally across the left knotting-cords, 1″ below the last row of knots. Tie the left knotting-cords around the left core-cord with Diagonal Double Half Hitches.

Step 12. Cut 2 green knotting-cords, each 27′ long. Fold the cords in half and mount them on the right and left core-cords with Clove Hitches.

Step 13. With the 4 center cords, tie 1 Square Knot directly below the Simple Overhand Knot tied in Step 9.

Step 14. Beginning with the 8 center cords, tie 7 rows of Alternating Square Knots.

Step 15. Cut 1 green core-cord 27′ long. Tie 1 Simple Overhand Knot in the center of the cord. Pin the Overhand Knot between the 2 center cords, ½″ below the last row of Alternating Square Knots. The left end of the green core-cord becomes the *left core-cord*. The right end of the green core-cord becomes the *right core-cord*. The 6 red and 6 green cords on the right become the *right core-cords*. The 6 red and 6 green cords on the left become the *left core-cords*.

Step 16. Carry the right core-cord horizontally across the right knotting-cords. Tie the right knotting-cords around the right core-cord with Horizontal Double Half Hitches.

Step 17. Carry the left core-cord horizontally across the left knotting-cords. Tie the left knotting-cords around the left core-cord with Horizontal Double Half Hitches.

Step 18. Fold the left core-cord down beside the left knotting-cords. Carry the right core-cord back across *all the knotting-cords and the left core-cord*, 1″ below the last row of knots. Tie all the knotting-cords and the left core-cord around the right core-cord with Horizontal Double Half Hitches.

Step 19. Carry the right core-cord back across the *left core-cord and all the knotting-cords*, 1″ below the last row of knots. Tie the left core-cord and all the knotting-cords around the right core-cord with Horizontal Double Half Hitches.

Step 20. Cut 1 green core-cord 27′ long. Fold the cord in half and mount it on the right core-cord between the 2 center Horizontal Double Half Hitches tied in Step 19.

Step 21. The 2 center cords become the *left* and *right core-cords*. The other 13 cords on the left become the *left knotting-cords*. The other 13 cords on the right become the *right knotting-cords*.

240

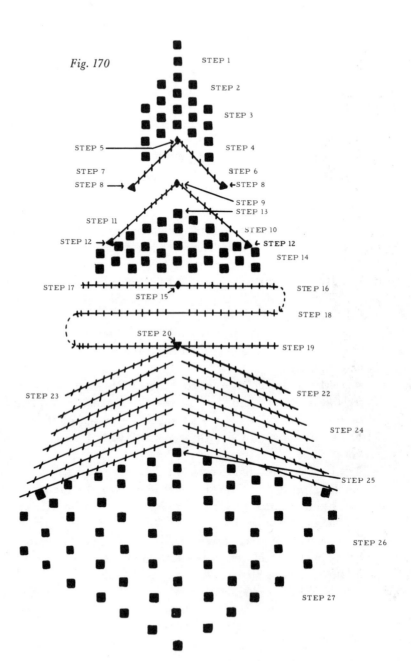

Fig. 170

STEP 1
STEP 2
STEP 3
STEP 4
STEP 5
STEP 6
STEP 7
STEP 8
STEP 8
STEP 9
STEP 13
STEP 11
STEP 10
STEP 12
STEP 12
STEP 14
STEP 17
STEP 16
STEP 15
STEP 18
STEP 20
STEP 19
STEP 23
STEP 22
STEP 24
STEP 25
STEP 26
STEP 27

Step 22. Carry the right core-cord diagonally across the right knotting-cords. Tie the right knotting-cords around the right core-cord with Diagonal Double Half Hitches.

Step 23. Carry the left core-cord diagonally across the left knotting-cords. Tie the left knotting-cords around the left core-cord with Diagonal Double Half Hitches.

Step 24. Repeat Steps 21, 22 and 23, six times, crossing the 2 center cords over one another before tying the rows of Diagonal Double Half Hitches.

Step 25. With the 4 center cords, tie 1 Square Knot, ½" below the center of the last row of knots.

Step 26. Tie 8 rows of Alternating Square Knots, leaving approximately ½" between each row of knots.

Step 27. Tie 6 more rows of Alternating Square Knots, *decreasing* each row by 1 Alternating Square Knot. Leave approximately ½" between each row of knots.

Step 28. Divide the number of cords in half. The outside left cord becomes the *left core-cord*. The other 13 cords on the left become the *left knotting-cords*. The outside right cord becomes the *right core-cord*. The other 13 cords on the right become the *right knotting-cords*.

Step 29. Carry the right core-cord diagonally across the right knotting-cords, 1½" below the last Alternating Square Knots. Tie the right knotting-cords around the right core-cord with Diagonal Double Half Hitches.

Step 30. Carry the left core-cord diagonally across the left knotting-cords, 1½" below the last Alternating Square Knots. Tie the right knotting-cords around the right core-cord with Diagonal Double Half Hitches. Cross the left core-cord over the right core-cord and tie the right core-cord around the left core-cord with Diagonal Double Half Hitches.

Step 31. Cut 6 red and 6 green knotting-cords, each 20' long. Fold all the knotting cords in half and mount them on the Step 28's *left core-cord*, between the Diagonal Double Half Hitches in the following sequence: 1 red Diagonal Double Half Hitch, 1 red knotting-cord, 2 red Diagonal Double Half Hitches, 1 red knotting-cord, 2 red Diagonal Double Half Hitches, 1 red knotting-cord, 2 green Diagonal Double Half Hitches, 1 green knotting-cord, 2 green Diagonal Double Half Hitches, 1 green knotting-cord, 2 green Diagonal Double Half Hitches, 1 green knotting-cord, 2 green Diagonal Double Half Hitches. Add new knotting-cords on the right side in the same manner.

Step 32. Divide the number of cords in half. The outside left cord becomes the *left core-cord*. The other 25 cords on the left become the *left knotting-cords*. The outside right cord becomes the *right core-cord*. The other 25 cords on the right become the *right knotting-cords*.

Step 33. Carry the right core-cord diagonally across the right knotting-cords. Tie the right knotting-cords around the right core-cord with Diagonal Double Half Hitches.

Fig. 171

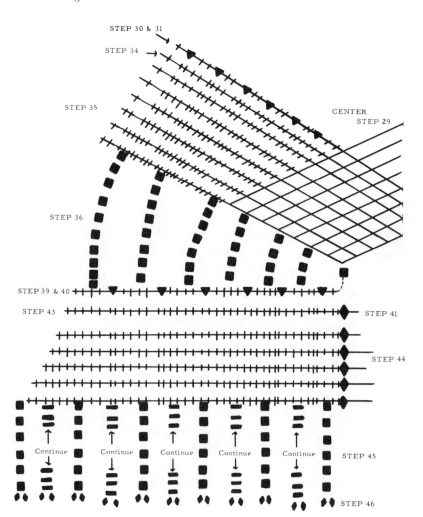

Fig. 172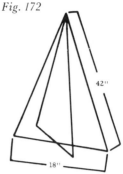

Step 34. Carry the left core-cord diagonally across the left knotting-cords. Tie the left knotting-cords around the left core-cord with Diagonal Double Half Hitches. Cross the left core-cord over the right core-cord. Tie the right core-cord around the left core-cord with 1 Diagonal Double Half Hitch.

Step 35. Repeat Steps 32, 33 and 34, six times.

Step 36. Divide the cords into groups of 4. Working from the left, tie the following number of Square Knots on each group of 4 cords: 10, 8, 7, 5, 4, 3, 1, 3, 4, 5, 7, 8, 10.

Step 37. The 2 center cords become the *left* and *right core-cords*. The other 25 cords on the left become the *left knotting-cords*. The other 25 cords on the right become the *right knotting-cords*.

Step 38. Carry the right core-cord horizontally across the right knotting-cords. Tie the right knotting-cords around the right core-cord with Horizontal Double Half Hitches.

Step 39. Carry the left core-cord horizontally across the left knotting-cords. Tie the left knotting-cords around the left core-cord with Horizontal Double Half Hitches.

Step 40. Cut 6 green and 6 red knotting-cords, each 8′ long. Fold all the knotting-cords in half, and mount on Step 37's *left core-cord*, between the Horizontal Double Half Hitches in the following sequence: 4 red Horizontal Double Half Hitches, 1 red knotting-cord, 4 green Horizontal Double Half Hitches, 1 green knotting cord, 4 green Horizontal Double Half Hitches, 1 green knotting-cord, 4 green Horizontal Double Half Hitches, 1 green knotting-cord, 2 green Horizontal Double Half Hitches, 2 red Horizontal Double Half Hitches, 1 red knotting-cord, 4 red Horizontal Double Half Hitches, 1 red knotting-cord, 1 red Horizontal Double Half Hitch. Add new knotting-cords on the right side in the same manner.

Step 41. Cut 1 red core-cord 8′ long. Tie 1 Simple Overhand Knot in the center of the cord. Pin the Overhand Knot between the 2 center cords. The left end of the red core-cord becomes the *left core-cord*. The right end of the red core-cord becomes the *right core-cord*. The other cords on the left become the *left knotting-cords*. The other cords on the right become the *right knotting-cords*.

Step 42. Carry the right core-cord horizontally across the right knotting-cords. Tie the right knotting-cords around the right core-cord with Horizontal Double Half Hitches. Fold the right core-cord down beside the right knotting-cords.

Step 43. Carry the left core-cord horizontally across the left knotting-cords. Tie the left knotting-cords around the left core-cord with Horizontal Double Half Hitches. Fold the left core-cord down beside the left knotting-cords.

Step 44. Repeat Steps 41, 42 and 43 five times.

Step 45. Divide the cords into groups of 4. On the 4 left cords, tie 6 Square Knots. Tie 6 Square Knots on every other group of 4 cords. Tie 12 Half Knots on the unknotted groups of 4 cords.

Step 46. Divide the cords into pairs. Tie 1 Double-Strand Overhand Knot on each pair of cords. Trim all ends to 2″. Untwist cord if bushy ends are desired.

Step 47. If a free-standing tree is desired, tie a second tree. Place the 2 knotted pieces together with the insides facing one another. Sew the 2 edges together. Place stitches between the knots so that the thread does not show. Build a frame of ¾″ lath *(See Fig. 172)*. Slide the tree over the frame and then trim it, if you wish.

Plate 63. Hanging Lamp. The interior lighting accents the patterns of the knots and the colors of the cords as well. A stunning chandelier could be made by combining three of these lamps.

HANGING LAMP

(5" by 24". See Figs. 173-175, Plate 63 and Color Plate XI)

MATERIALS

    2 metal rings, 1" in diameter; 1 plastic or fiber glass lampshade cylinder, 5" by 22"; 3-prong spider set; lamp fixture; cord; 600' rust Lily Jute-Tone; 300' gold Lily Jute-Tone.

METHOD

Step 1. Assemble the spider set and attach to lampshade. Cut 12 rust cords, each 25' long. Fold all the cords in half and mount them on one of the metal rings with Clove Hitches. Divide the cords into groups of 4. Tie 14 Square Knots on each group of 4 cords. Tape the last 5 Square Knots of each sinnet to the top outside of the lampshade, spacing them equal distance apart, between the ends of the spider set.

Step 2. Cut 12 rust and 12 gold cords, each 25' long. Fold all the cords in half and mount them on the 2nd metal ring with Clove Hitches in the following sequence: 4 rust, 4 gold, 4 rust, 4 gold, 4 rust, 4 gold.

Step 3. Divide the cords into groups, keeping the colors separate. Steps 4 through 7 will be worked on 1 group of rust cords.

Step 4. With the 4 center cords, tie 1 Square Knot. Tie 10 rows of Alternating Square Knots.

Step 5. Divide the cords into groups of 4. On each group of 4 cords, tie 24 Half Knots.

Step 6. With the 4 center cords, tie 12 Square Knots. With the 2 left cords, tie 14 Single Chain Knots. With the 2 right cords, tie 14 Single Chain Knots.

Step 7. Beginning with the outside 4 cords on either side, tie 1 row of Square Knots. Tie 7 rows of Alternating Square Knots.

Step 8. Repeat Steps 4 through 7 on the other 2 groups of rust cords.

Step 9. Repeat Steps 4 through 6 on the 3 groups of gold cords.

Step 10. Steps 11, 12 and 13 will be worked on 1 group of gold cords.

Step 11. Beginning with the outside 4 cords on either side, tie 1 row of Square Knots. Tie 4 rows of Alternating Square Knots.

Step 12. Place the 2 center cords on either side of 1 of the spider prongs. Directly below the spider prong, with the 4 center cords, tie 1 Square Knot.

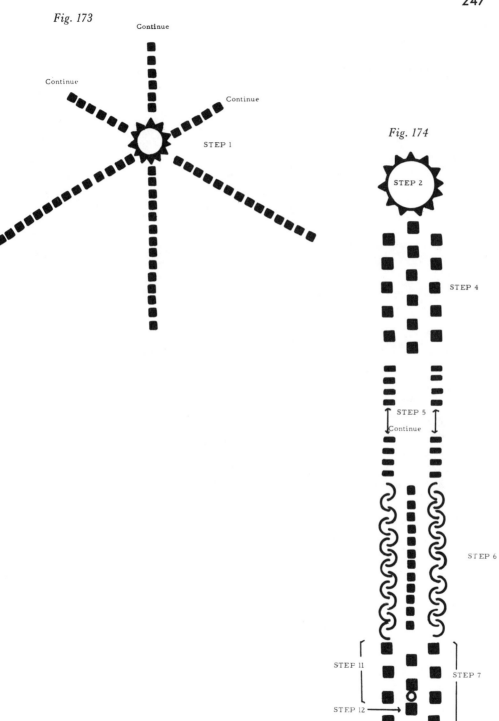

Fig. 173

Continue

Continue

Continue

STEP 1

Fig. 174

STEP 2

STEP 4

STEP 5

Continue

STEP 6

STEP 11

STEP 7

STEP 12

STEP 13

Step 13. Tie 2 rows of Alternating Square Knots.

Step 14. Repeat Steps 11, 12 and 13 on the other 2 groups of gold cords.

Step 15. Place the 3 groups of rust cords tied in Steps 4 through 8 between the 6 groups of rust cords tied in Step 1. Tape these rust cords in place.

Step 16. Beginning with 2 rust and 2 gold cords, tie 1 row of Alternating Square Knots around the lampshade. This row of knots will join all the groups of cords together.

Step 17. Tie 3 rows of Alternating Square Knots.

Step 18. Divide the cords into 6 groups, keeping the gold separate from the rust.

Step 19. This step will be worked on 1 group of gold cords. With the 4 center cords, tie 7 Square Knots. With the 2 left cords, tie 9 Single Chain Knots. With the 2 right cords, tie 9 Single Chain Knots.

Step 20. Repeat Step 19 on the other 2 groups of gold cords.

Step 21. Steps 22 through 27 will be worked on 1 group of rust cords.

Step 22. Tie 1 row of Alternating Square Knots.

Step 23. With the 8 center cords, tie 2 Alternating Square Knots.

Step 24. With the 4 center cords, tie 1 Alternating Square Knot.

Step 25. Divide the number of cords in half. The outside left cord becomes the *left core-cord*. The other 7 cords on the left become the *left knotting-cords*. The outside right cord becomes the *right core-cord*. The other 7 cords on the right become the *right knotting-cords*.

Step 26. Carry the right core-cord diagonally across the right knotting-cords. Tie the right knotting-cords around the right core-cord with Diagonal Double Half Hitches.

Step 27. Carry the left core-cord diagonally across the left knotting-cords. Tie the left knotting-cords around the left core-cord with Diagonal Double Half Hitches.

Step 28. Repeat Steps 22 through 27 on the other 2 groups of rust cords.

Step 29. Beginning with 2 rust and 2 gold cords, tie 1 row of 5 Square Knots on each group of rust cords.

Step 30. Tie 3 rows of Alternating Square Knots around the lampshade. The top row of knots will join all the groups of cords together.

Step 31. Repeat Step 29.

Step 32. With each group of rust cords, tie 1 row of 4 Alternating Square Knots.

Step 33. With the 12 center rust cords of each group, tie 1 row of 3 Alternating Square Knots.

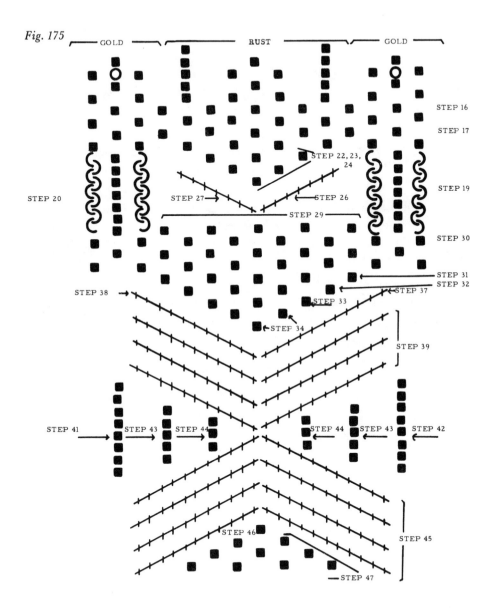

Fig. 175

Step 34. Repeat Steps 23 and 24.

Step 35. Divide all the cords into 3 groups. The colors in each group should be in the following sequence: 4 gold; 16 rust; 4 gold. Steps 36 through 39 will be worked on 1 group of cords.

Step 36. Divide the number of cords in half. The outside left cord becomes the *left core-cord*. The other 11 cords on the left become the *left knotting-cords*. The outside right cord becomes the *right core-cord*. The other 11 cords on the right become the *right knotting-cords*.

Step 37. Carry the right core-cord diagonally across the right knotting-cords. Tie the right knotting-cords around the right core-cord with Diagonal Double Half Hitches.

Step 38. Carry the left core-cord diagonally across the left knotting-cords. Tie the left knotting-cords around the left core-cord with Diagonal Double Half Hitches. Cross the left core-cord over the right core-cord. Tie the right core-cord around the left core-cord with 1 Diagonal Double Half Hitch.

Step 39. Repeat Steps 36, 37 and 38 three times.

Step 40. Repeat Steps 36 through 39 on the other 2 groups of cords.

Step 41. With 2 rust cords from 1 group of cords, and 2 rust cords from a 2nd group of cords, tie 8 Square Knots.

Step 42. Repeat Step 41 between each group of cords.

Step 43. With the 4 cords on either side of the knots tied in Steps 41 and 42, tie 5 Square Knots.

Step 44. With the next 4 cords beside the knots tied in Step 43, tie 3 Square Knots.

Step 45. Repeat Steps 35 through 40.

Step 46. With 2 rust cords from 1 group of cords, and 2 rust cords from a 2nd group of cords, tie 1 Square Knot.

Step 47. Tie 3 rows of Alternating Square Knots below the Square Knot tied in Step 46.

Step 48. Trim all ends to 3".

Step 49. Insert the cord and lamp fixture up through the shade, spider prong and both rings. Make a knot in the cord to support the top ring. Use only a small wattage bulb so that you will not burn the jute.

SOURCES OF SUPPLY

In addition to the following suppliers, you will find cord and yarn for macrame in Art Needlework shops, the Art Needlework department in department stores, and even a few of the cords in your local hardware store.

American Handicrafts, 18-20 West 14th Street, New York, N.Y. 10011.

Barnes & Blake, Ltd., P.O. Box 2387, New York, N.Y. 10001.

Condon & Sons, Ltd., 65 Queen Street, Charlottetown, P.O. Box 129, Prince Edward Island, Canada.

Craft Yarns of Rhode Island, Inc., 603 Mineral Spring Ave., Pawtucket, R.I. 02860.

Frederick J. Fawcett, Inc., 129 South Street, Boston, Mass. 02111.

Fibre Yarn Co., Inc., 840 Sixth Avenue, New York, N.Y. 10001.

Greenberg & Hammer, Inc., 24 West 57th Street, New York, N.Y. 10022.

P.C. Herwig Company, 246 Clinton Street, Brooklyn, N.Y. 11201.

Lily Mills Co., Shelby, N.C. 28150.

Magnolia Weaving, 2635 29th West, Seattle, Wash. 98199.

Paternayan Bros., Inc. (Wholesale only), 312 East 95th Street, New York, N.Y. 10038.

Mrs. Lyle B. Robinson, 1019 N.E. 62nd, Seattle, Wash. 98115.

I.B. Silk Co., 315 West 36th Street, New York, N.Y. 10018.

Troy Yarn and Textile Company, Pawtucket, R.I. 02860.

Walbead, 38 West 37th Street, New York, N.Y. 10018.

Walco Products (Wholesale only), 1200 Zerega Ave., Bronx, N.Y. 10400.

William and Company, Box 318, Madison Square Station, New York, N.Y. 10010.

The Yarn Depot, 545 Sutter Street, San Francisco, Calif. 94102.

Adding cords with square knots, 54
Alternating knots
    half hitch, 46, 58
    overhand knot, 53, 58
    reversed double half hitch, 51, 59
    square knot, 54, 58
Appliqué tote bag, 144

Bags
    cable cord, 133
    rayon, 138
    sisal tote, 141, 142
    tote, appliqué, 144
    wool, 135
Banded
    belt, 68
    sash, 81
Beaded
    bottle cover, 174
    choker, 96
    jute belt, 70
    jute sash, 92
    rayon necklace, 98
    tunic, 150
Beads, threading, 25, 26
Bells of India wall hanging, 194, 196
Belts
    banded, 68
    beaded jute, 70
    cable cord, 74
    diamond patterns, 65, 66
    double triangle, 64
    suede, 78
    wide jute, 72
Boards, for knotting, 10
Bobbin, make a, 22
Bookmarkers
    diamond pattern, 169
    giant "X", 170
    striped, 173

Bottle covers
    beaded, 174
    jute, 179
    rayon, 180
Bracelets
    cable cord, 119
    rayon, 121
    seashell, 117
Braided pillow top, 184
Butterfly, 22

Cable cord, 35
    bag, 133
    belt, 74
    bracelet, 119
    key ring, 130
Chevron
    pillow top, 186
    sash, 86
Chokers
    simple beaded, 96
    triangle, 94
    zigzag, 95
Christmas tree, 236
Clamps, 16
Cleaning projects, 32
Clove hitch, 40, 58
Cords
    adding fringe, 28
    adding with square knots, 54
    cable, 35
    cotton yarn, 37
    ending, 27
    jute, 34
    knitting yarn, 37
    measuring with clamps, 17
    nylon seine, 35
    polypropylene, 37
    rattail, 37
    rayon, 37

sisal, 35
substituting, 34
tension on, 18
types of, 34
wool rug yarn, 37
Core-cord, 40
Cotton yarn, 37

Diagonal double half hitch, 48, 58
Diamond pattern
belt, 65, 66
bookmarker, 169
of diagonal double half hitches, 55, 59
pillow top, 189
sash, 88
tunic, 153
Double chain knot, 52, 59
Double half hitch
alternating, 46, 58
alternating reversed, 51, 59
diagonal, 48, 58
horizontal, 46, 58
reversed, 51, 59
vertical, 49, 58
Double triangle belt, 64, 65
Dyeing, materials needed, 29, 30
Dyes
commercial, 28
natural, 29, 30

Ending cords, 25, 27
Eyeglass cases
jute, 127
leaf pattern, 123
striped, 126

Free-standing Christmas tree, 237
Fringes, adding with hook, 28

Giant "X" bookmarker, 170
Glue
for ends, 24
splicing with, 25

Half hitch, 46, 58
Half knot, 42, 58

Handles, pinning, 21
Hanging lamp, 245
Holding-cord, 40
pinning, 21
Hooks, 28

Indian jute necklace, 110
Interlocking square knot, 54, 59

Jute, 34
beaded belt, 70
beaded sash, 92
bottle cover, 179
eyeglass case, 127
key ring, 132
necklace, Indian, 110
lacy, 104
plant hanger, 165
sash, lacy, 76
wall hanging, 213
wide belt, 72

Key rings
cable cord, 130
jute, 132
rattail, 129
Knitting yarn, 37
Knots
alternating double half hitch, 46, 58
alternating half hitch, 46, 58
alternating overhand knot, 53, 58
alternating reversed double half hitch, 51, 59
alternating square, 53, 59
clove hitch, 41, 58
diagonal double half hitch, 48, 58
double chain, 52, 59
half hitch, 45, 58
half knot, 42, 58
horizonal double half hitch, 46, 58
interlocking square, 54, 59
overhand knot, 41, 58
reversed double half hitch, 51, 59
single chain knot, 52, 59
square knot, 43, 58
symbols, 58, 59

tying, in multicolored projects, 39
vertical double half hitch, 49, 58
Knotting boards, 10
  acoustic tiles, 11
  bricks, 14
  bulletin boards, 11
  clipboard, 13
  composition board, 11
  corrugated cardboard, 13
  foam rubber padding, 13
  foam rubber squares, 11
  marking with guidelines, 15
  rubber pads, 13
  sizes, 15
  wooden, 14
Knotting-cord, 40
Knotting sample, 62

Lacy jute
  necklace, 104
  sash, 76
Lamp, 245
Leaf pattern eyeglass case, 123
Lengths of cords, determining, 32

Materials, 9
Measuring cords with clamps, 17
Methods, 9
Multicolored projects, knot tying, 39
Multiple cords, square knot with, 44

Necklaces
  beaded rayon, 98
  Indian jute, 110
  lacy jute, 104
  party, 101, 102
  wool, 106
Needles, 27
Nylon
  plant hanger, 163
  seine twine, 35

Overhand knot, 41, 58

Party necklace, 101, 102
Party tunic, 146

Pillow tops
  braided, 184
  chevron, 186
  diamond, 189
  square knot, 182
Pinning
  holding-cords, 21
  rings, tubes, handles, etc., 21
  symmetrical patterns, 21
Pins, 19
Plant hangers
  jute, 165
  nylon, 163
  sisal, 167
Polypropylene cord, 37

Radiating bands sash, 90
Rattail, 37
  key ring, 129
Rayon cord, 37
  bag, 138
  bottle cover, 180
  bracelet, 121
  necklace, 98
Reversed double half hitch, 51, 59
Rings, pinning, 21, 22
Room divider, 192

Sample of knotting, 62
Sampler, 33
Sashes
  banded, 81
  beaded jute, 92
  chevron, 86
  diamond, 88
  lacy jute, 76
  radiating bands, 90
  simple, 71
  triple "V", 84
  "V", 82
Scarecrow wall hanging, 229
Seashell bracelet, 117
Shears, 27, 28
Simple beaded choker, 96
Simple sash, 71
Single chain knot, 52, 59
Sinnet, 40

Sisal, 35
    plant hanger, 167
    and shell wall hanging, 199
    tote bag, 141, 142
    wall hanging, 222
Splicing cords, 25
Square knot, 43, 58
    adding cords with, 54
    alternating, 53
    interlocking, 54
    pillow top, 182
    with multiple cords, 44
Striped bookmarker, 173
Striped eyeglass case, 126
Suede belt, 78
Suspenders, 115
Symbols for knots, 58, 59
Symmetrical patterns, pinning, 21

Tape
    beginning with, 24
    for ends, 24
Tension on cords, 18
Threading beads, 25, 26
Tie-dyeing, 29, 32
Tote bag
    appliqué, 144
    sisal, 141, 142
"T" pins, 19
Triangle choker, 94
Triangle pattern of diagonal double
    half hitches, 59

Triple "V" sash, 84
Tubes, pinning, 21
Tunics
    beaded, 150
    diamond, 153
    party, 146

Vertical double half hitch, 49, 58
Vest, 156
"V" sash, 82

Wall hangings
    bells of India, 194, 196
    Christmas tree, 236
    jute, 213
    scarecrow, 229
    sisal, 222
    sisal and shell, 199
    wool, 206
Wax, for ends, 24
Wide jute belt, 72
Wool
    bag, 135
    necklace, 106
    rug yarn, 37
    wall hanging, 206

"X" pattern
    of diagonal double half hitches, 56,
    59

Zigzag choker, 95